Bede Griffiths

THE MARRIAGE
OF EAST AND WEST

A Sequel To
The Golden String

Templegate Publishers
Springfield, Illinois

Made and printed in the United States by:

Templegate Publishers
302 East Adams Street
P.O. Box 5152
Springfield, Illinois 62705
(217) 522-3353

ISBN 0-87243-105-3

Books by Bede Griffiths:
  The Golden String
  The Marriage of East and West
  The Cosmic Revelation
  Christ in India
  Return to the Center
  A New Vision of Reality
  The New Creation in Christ
  Modern Spirituality Series: Bede Griffiths

CONTENTS

I

The Discovery of India

When I wrote *The Golden String*,[1] telling the story of my search for God, which led me to the Catholic Church and to a Benedictine monastery, I thought that I had reached the end of my journey, at least as far as this world was concerned. But in fact, even while I was writing *The Golden String*, a new era was about to begin in my life, which was to bring about changes, as profound as any that had gone before. I had been led to the discovery first of God, then of Christ, and finally of the Church. But now I have been led in a strange way to retrace the path I had taken and to make new discoveries about God, about Christ and about the Catholic Church. It was as though I had been climbing a mountain, and having reached the peak, discovered further ranges beyond with new peaks, opening up a new horizon.

All this came about through my meeting with an Indian Benedictine monk, who was planning to make a monastic foundation in India. For years I had been studying the Vedanta and had begun to realize its significance for the Church and the world. Now I was given the opportunity to go to the source of this tradition, to live in India and discover the secret of the wisdom of India. It was not merely the desire for new ideas which drew me to India, but the desire for a new way of life. I remember writing to a friend at the time: 'I want to discover the other half of my soul.' I had begun to find that there was something lacking not only in the Western world but in the Western Church. We were living from one half of our soul, from the conscious, rational level and we needed to discover the other half, the unconscious, intuitive dimension. I wanted to experience in my life the marriage of these two dimensions of human existence, the rational and intuitive, the conscious and unconscious, the masculine and feminine. I wanted to find the way to the marriage of East and West.

My discovery began even before I reached India. I travelled by boat and I remember how at my first encounter with the East, at Port Said and Aden, I was fascinated with the spectacle of this world of immeasurable beauty and vitality. It was not the beauty of nature which struck me now, but the beauty of human nature, of what Blake called the 'human form divine'. It was the same when I reached Bombay. It was not the poverty and the misery which struck me so much as the sheer beauty and vitality of the people. On all sides was a swarming mass of humanity, children running about quite naked, women in saris, men with turbans, everywhere displaying the beauty of the human form. Whether sitting or standing or walking there was grace in all their movements and I felt that I was in the presence of a hidden power of nature. I explained it to myself by saying that these people were living from the 'unconscious'. People in the West are dominated by the conscious mind; they go about their business each shut up in his own ego. There is a kind of fixed determination in their minds, which makes their movements and gestures stiff and awkward, and they all tend to wear the same drab clothes. But in the East people live not from the conscious mind but from the unconscious, from the body not from the mind. As a result they have the natural spontaneous beauty of flowers and animals, and their dress is as varied and colourful as that of a flower-garden.

Often, looking down on the scene at a railway platform, I have thought that it looked like a flower-garden, the women with their brightly-coloured saris sitting in circles here and there, the children running about with movements and gestures of spontaneous joy. After all these years in India this remains my deepest impression. There is poverty and misery enough in India, but above all in the villages and among the poorest there is an abundance of life and joy.

But, of course, this is not a merely animal life and beauty, it has the grace of human intelligence. They live from the unconscious, but it is the human unconscious, what Jung has called the anima as opposed to the animus. Every human being is both masculine and feminine. In the man the masculine aspect, the animus, is normally dominant, and in the woman the feminine or anima. In every person a certain balance or harmony has to be achieved, but in the West today the masculine aspect, the rational, active, aggressive power of the mind, is dominant, while in the East the feminine aspect, the intuitive, passive, sympathetic power of the mind is dominant. The future of the world depends on the 'marriage' of these two minds, the conscious and the unconscious, the rational and the intuitive, the active and the passive. In India and all over the world today these two minds are meeting, but often the impact of the West on the East is that of a violent aggression, whether by armed power as in the past, or by the much more subtle aggression of science and technology exploiting man and nature, as at present.

The present system of industrialism in the West is the product of the violent, aggressive, rational mind of the West – whether organized in a capitalist or a socialist system makes no difference, except that the latter tends to be more oppressive and inhuman – which can only lead to the destruction of the ancient cultures of the East. Yet it still remains possible to conceive of a development of science and technology which would seek not to dominate nature in the style of the West but to work with nature, building up from the basis of the village economy, as Mahatma Gandhi sought to do, and so create a new culture, in which man and nature, reason and intuition, the Yang and the Yin in Chinese terms, would be brought into harmony.

But there is something more in Indian culture than a search for harmony between man and nature, conscious and unconscious; there is a profound awareness of a power beyond both man and nature which penetrates everything and is the real source of the beauty and vitality of Indian life. I realized this most clearly when I visited the Cave of Elephanta outside Bombay. The cave has a forest of pillars inside it, not uncommon in Hindu temples, which creates an atmosphere of mystery and immensity, and as you approach, the great figure of Siva Maheswara – the Great God – with his three faces, representing his benign and terrible and contemplative aspects, looms out of the darkness from a recess in the wall. It is colossal and overwhelming at first, but when you look into the front face you see that it is in deep contemplation. There is absolute peace there, infinitely distant yet infinitely near, solemn, benign, gentle and majestic. Here carved in stone is the very genius of India and the East. This is what I had come to India to find, this contemplative dimension of human existence, which the West has almost lost and the East is losing. Here engraved in stone one could encounter that hidden depth of existence, springing from the depth of nature and the unconscious, penetrating all human existence and going beyond into the mystery of the infinite and eternal, not as something remote and inaccessible, but as something almost tangible engraved in this stone. Here was the secret I had come to discover. The mind of the East is open not only to man and nature in an intuitive understanding, but also to that hidden Power which pervades both man and nature and reveals to those who are attuned to it the real meaning of human existence.

If the West as a whole has lost this intuitive awareness of the presence of God in man and nature, the Church in the West is faced with the same problem. Christianity was originally an Eastern religion (like practically all religions), but its movement from the beginning has been predominantly westwards. It passed with St Paul through Asia Minor to Greece and Rome, and then in the course of time to Europe and America. As a result, though always retaining its Eastern basis it has become a Western religion. Its theology is Greek, its organization Roman, its cultural expression European.

This was immediately evident in Bombay. The churches are either Gothic or Baroque; the statues and pictures are from European models; altars and candlesticks and stained glass are often imported from abroad. Everything is done to make the Church appear foreign to India. Yet the Indian people somehow manage to transform even these artificial buildings. They swarm everywhere, pressing up against the altar rails and through the doors and windows, overwhelming the Victorian propriety of the churches with their spontaneous vitality.

Yet this, of course, is on a superficial level. The Indian Church has to undergo a radical transformation, if it is ever to respond to the needs of the Indian people. It has to rethink its theology in Indian instead of Greek terms, and to adapt its organization to Indian instead of Roman models. Even its Semitic base cannot go untouched. Christianity shares with Judaism and Islam a Semitic structure of language and thought. It has to learn to see this Semitic tradition with all its unique values in the light of the Oriental tradition, to learn what Hinduism, Buddhism, Taoism and Confucianism have to teach it. Then only will the 'marriage' take place in the Church as in the world between East and West.

It was only gradually that this realization came to me. When we arrived in Bangalore, we bought a property some miles outside Bangalore in a village called Kengeri and there we began our monastic life. At this time, though I wanted to continue the study of Indian thought, I had no idea of changing our style of life. We wore the traditional Benedictine habit. We built a chapel in Western style, with chairs and reading desks. We had our meals sitting at table with spoons, knives and forks. Our cells were simply furnished with wooden beds and straw mattresses, a table, a chair and a shelf for clothes and books. This was what I then considered a model of simplicity. It was only gradually that I discovered that nearly all these things were unheard-of luxuries in the neighbouring village. A few rich people might have tables and chairs and even a radio or a gramophone, but most of the villagers normally sat on the floor, ate with their hands from a plantain leaf, and slept on a mat on the floor.

Thus I gradually became aware of a standard of poverty and simplicity which was far beyond anything which I had imagined in Europe. At the same time I realized that this poverty and simplicity did not mean that the people were any less cultured. There was an old man in the village who was a Sanskrit scholar, and from him I learned much of the traditional Hindu wisdom. There were also several students studying at the university, well acquainted with Western ways, one of whom became one of my closest friends. He was Western-minded in many ways and admired Western culture, but he had no difficulty in sitting on the floor for his meals and eating with his hand, and every week without fail he would visit the little temple of the monkey god Hanuman near our monastery and conduct the worship there. So I began to realize how a primeval religion and culture could exist side by side with Western ways.

At this time I was studying Sanskrit with Raimundo Panikkar, who embodies in a unique way this meeting of East and West. His mother was a Spanish Catholic and his father came from a well-known Hindu family. He had been brought up in Europe, had taken degrees in science, philosophy and theology, and had now come to India to discover his Indian heritage. Together we explored this Indian culture which was now beginning to unfold before my eyes. We spent some weeks together visiting the temples in the old Mysore State.[2]

At the very beginning there was an unforgettable experience, when we were invited by a man whom we met on the way to visit his home. He took us to a tiny two-roomed cottage, where we sat cross-legged on the floor, and two little boys gave us a concert of Indian classical music. There was no furniture in the house. One little boy was lying ill on a mat on the floor and the others sat beside us, one playing a stringed instrument and both singing together, beating the time with their hands and completely absorbed in the music. The mother prepared tea in the kitchen, which we drank from small brass vessels, but later she too came and played and sang herself. The father explained to us the meaning of the songs, which were either in Sanskrit or one of the south Indian languages, and were all, of course, religious. So there we were sitting on the floor in this little cottage with no modern conveniences, brought face to face with one of the most profound religious cultures of the world.

Our visits to the temples only confirmed this impression. At Belur, Halebid and Somnathpur we found architecture

and sculpture of a beauty and refinement equal to the finest
Gothic art, but beyond the outward form of beauty there was
the deep inner meaning of the temples.

Halebid in particular was a most enchanting place, an old
temple set in a lovely valley with a broad river flowing by,
reminding one of Tintern or Fountains. Round the outside
of the temple there are sculptured friezes in ascending order,
representing first the animal world – elephants, horses, birds
– then the human world with stories from the Hindu epics,
the *Ramayana* and *Mahabharata*, and finally the divine world,
the world of the gods and goddesses. It was a manifestation of
the cosmic mystery in stone, the divine life manifesting itself
in the three worlds, the animal, the human and the divine.

Another impression of lasting significance was the figure
of a naked man standing upright to be found in many of the
Jain temples here, above all the colossal figure in the temple at
Sravan Belgola. This, I believe, is the figure of Purusha, the
Primeval Man, the Archetypal Man, who appears in the Rig
Veda, of whom it is said that he contains the whole creation
in himself. 'Three quarters of him is above in heaven, one
quarter is here on earth.' This is akin to the Adam Kadmon,
the first Adam, of Jewish tradition and the Universal Man of
Muslim tradition. When Jesus called himself the Son of Man
he was relating himself to this primeval tradition and
revealing the underlying unity of religions. Thus the temples
in Mysore revealed Hinduism as the Cosmic religion, the
religion of God's revelation in the Cosmos and in Man.

But perhaps no less significant was the impression made
when we sat down by the river beside a little shrine, in which
there was nothing but a roughly-carved lingam and yoni –
the male and female organs. A European would be inclined to
regard this as 'obscene' but for a Hindu it has no such
significance. For the Hindu sex is essentially 'holy'. It is a

manifestation of the divine life and is to be worshipped like any other form of the divinity. God manifests himself in all the works of nature, in earth and fire and air and water, in plant and animal and man. Sex is one of the manifestations of the divine power – the Sakti – which sustains the universe and has the character of a sacrament.

It is this vision of a cosmic unity, in which man and nature are sustained by an all-pervading spirit, which the West needs to learn from the East. It is this that explains the extraordinary sacredness which attaches to every created thing in India. The earth is sacred, and no ploughing or sowing or reaping can take place without some religious rite. Eating is a sacred action and every meal is conceived as a sacrifice to God. Water is sacred and no religious Hindu will take a bath without invoking the sacred power of the water, which descends from heaven and, caught on the head of Siva, is distributed in the fertilizing streams of the Ganges and other rivers. Air is sacred, the breath of life which comes from God and sustains all living creatures. Fire is sacred, especially in its source in the sun, which brings light and life to all creatures. So also with plants and trees, especially certain plants like the tulsi plant and certain trees like the banyan. Animals are sacred, especially the cow, which gives her milk as a mother, but also the elephant, the monkey and the snake. Finally man is sacred; every man is a manifestation of God but especially a holy man, in whom the divine presence can be more clearly seen.

This is the sacred universe, in which man has lived as far as we know from the beginning of history and which has been completely demolished by the Western scientific world. Every trace of sacredness has been removed from life so that Western man finds himself in a universe in which both man and nature have been deprived of any ultimate meaning.

There are some who think that this process of secularization, which has abolished the sacred order of the ancient religions, is itself the effect of the Christian revelation, which placed the whole creation under the dominion of the one supreme God and took away the power of the 'gods'. It is true that the tendency of the Cosmic religion in all its forms is to deify the powers of nature and so to make man subject to what St Paul called the 'cosmic powers', but this is not the authentic tradition of Oriental religion whether Hindu, Buddhist or Taoist. In all these religions the powers of nature or the 'gods' are held to be subject to the one supreme Being, by whatever name it may be known. In Hinduism it has always been held that the 'gods' are but names and forms of the one Being, who has no name or form. Moreover, Christianity in rejecting the 'gods' of Greece and Rome did not make the world any less sacred but on the contrary made everything without exception sacred, because of its living relation to God its creator. The degradation of the Western world has come not from Christianity (except, perhaps, in some of its more debased forms), but from the rejection of the very idea of God.

The difference between the Semitic religions (Judaism, Christianity and Islam) and the Oriental religions (Hinduism, Buddhism and Taoism) seems to lie in this; that in the Semitic tradition God is represented as the transcendent Lord of creation, infinitely 'holy', that is separate from and above nature, and never to be confused with it. But in the Oriental tradition God – or the Absolute, by whatever word it may be named – is immanent in all creation. The world does not exist apart from God but 'in' God; he dwells in the heart of every creature. The danger of this position is that God is very easily confused with nature; the transcendent aspect of Being is lost sight of and the result is pantheism. In the same way since

God is conceived as present in everything, in the evil as well as the good, the distinction between good and evil is easily lost.

But perhaps the greatest weakness in the Oriental tradition is that the material world tends to be regarded as an illusion – as *maya* – the product of 'ignorance' (*avidya*). The world of ordinary experience is held to have only an apparent reality and in the ultimate state of 'knowledge' (*paravidya*) all differences disappear and the one, absolute reality alone remains.

When I first came to India I encountered this doctrine among almost all the educated Hindus with whom I talked, who all claimed to follow the teaching of the great Sankaracharya. But further study and experience has convinced me that this is not the teaching of the Upanishads or the Bhagavad Gita, and the doctrine of Sankara himself is far more subtle and profound than it is often made out to be. The authentic Hindu tradition does not deny the reality of the material world. It sees the whole creation as pervaded by the one, eternal Spirit, who creates, sustains and finally dissolves the world, and this all-pervading Spirit – the Brahman – is no less transcendent than immanent. It is 'unseen, inconceivable, unimaginable, indescribable'. Of every name and form which may be given to this supreme Being, we have to say: not this, not this – *neti, neti*.

This Hinduism starting from the immanence of God in creation ascends to the awareness of his infinite transcendence, and in the same way the Hebrew-Christian tradition starting from the infinite transcendence of God or Yahweh sees this God descending to earth, manifesting himself through his angels, speaking his Word to his prophets and finally becoming 'incarnate' – the Word became flesh – and communicating his Spirit to man.

The true character of this original Semitic tradition was brought home to me when I left Bangalore and settled in Kerala. We were unable to make the foundation which we had planned in Kengeri, and I was invited by a Cistercian monk, Father Francis Mahieu, to join in making a foundation[3] in Kerala. I had now realized that it was necessary to change our style of life, if we were to enter into the authentic tradition of Indian culture, and we now adopted the *kavi* habit of the Hindu *sannyasi* – one who renounces the world in order to seek for God – which corresponds in India to the vocation of the Christian monk.

We also followed the normal customs of the *sannyasi*, going barefoot, sitting on the floor both for meals and for prayer, eating with the hands, and sleeping on a mat. We were therefore able to come nearer to the condition of the poor man in India. This was assisted by the fact that when we began our monastic life in Kerala, we were compelled to live in a palm-leaf hut. The stone building, which we were erecting, was not yet complete and we had to spend the whole of the monsoon season, with nearly two hundred inches of rain, in this frail hut. Yet we found that we were able to survive even under these conditions. The floor of the hut, which was made of earth, became so damp that we had to cover it first with straw and then with planks in order to keep dry. But apart from this, we were also able to continue our monastic life, celebrating the 'Qurbana', the Eucharist in the Syrian rite, which we had adopted, chanting the prayer, continuing our study and doing all the necessary work without a break.

I shall always be thankful that I was able to experience not only something of the hardships but also the joy in simplicity of the poor man in India. I remember that when I first saw the little huts in which the people live in the villages I wondered how it was possible for human beings to live under such conditions. But experience has taught me that the simple mud hut with a thatched roof, with no furniture and no conveniences, is sufficient for all basic human needs and can bring more peace and joy than many of the houses of the rich. I thus began to understand the meaning of the words of the Gospel: 'Blessed are you poor, blessed are you that mourn, blessed are you that are hungry.' The poor of India suffer and go hungry, but they have a blessing on their lives which the Western world has lost.

When we came to Kerala, we adopted the Syrian rite, to which the majority of Christians in Kerala belong. The Christian faith is said to have been brought to India by the apostle Thomas, and there has certainly been a church in Kerala from a very early time. The earliest historical evidence points to a Church existing in India from at least the fourth century and forming part of the Persian or East Syrian Church. It is often forgotten that while the Christian Church was spreading westwards, through Asia Minor to Greece and Rome, it was also spreading eastwards through Syria and Mesopotamia. The centre of this Eastern Church was the city of Edessa on the borders of Syria and Mesopotamia, which spoke a form of Aramaic, the language of Jesus and his disciples, which came to be known as Syriac. This Syrian Church spread in the following centuries through Persia to China and India and had hundreds of churches and monasteries throughout this region. Unfortunately, it adopted a 'Nestorian' form of the Christian faith, which was rejected by the Council of Chalcedon, and thus became separated from the Churches of the West. Yet it represents a remarkable witness to an Oriental form of Christianity, which has its value to the present day. Later this Syrian Christianity was overwhelmed by the forces of Islam and only small pockets remain today in the Middle East as relics of a once-great Church.

In Kerala, on the other hand, this Syrian Church survives in greater strength than any other Christian Church, but unfortunately, the divisions of Western Christendom are reflected in it. There are Syrian Catholics, Syrian Orthodox and Syrian Protestants, and to complicate matters there is an earlier division of the Syrian Church, which took place in the fifth century when the East Syrians with their centre in Persia adopted the 'Nestorian' form of the Christian faith with its emphasis on the human nature of Christ, while the West Syrians with their centre in Antioch adopted the 'Monophysite' form of faith with its emphasis on the divine nature in Christ.

When we decided to make our foundation in Kerala, we adopted the West Syrian rite of Antioch, the Malankara rite, as it is known in Kerala, as being a more purely Oriental rite, the East Syrian, or Malabar rite, having been much Latinized as is often the way with the Eastern Churches which are united with Rome. We were thus faced from the outset with all those tragic divisions which have plagued the Christian Churches from the earliest times. In a sense, of course, these divisions are perfectly normal and natural. It is normal and right that the Christian faith should find a different expression in both East and West, and that there should be further divisions based on local differences in the expression of faith and worship. What is tragic is that each of these Churches should have contended that its own form of faith and worship was the true form and should have condemned all others as opposed to the true faith. Today we realize that the one Faith can have different forms of expression in theology and liturgy and organization, and each can learn to appreciate the particular witness of the other Churches.

The Syrian liturgy and theology to which we were introduced in Kerala is something of extraordinary interest. It is first of all an Oriental form of Christianity, which though it owes something to the Greek world through its centre in Antioch, remains rooted in the Semitic world of the Middle East. It belongs, in fact, to the same world as the Bible itself. It is as though it sprang from the same soil as the Bible, using the same language as was used in Palestine and expressing itself not in the metaphysical terms of Greek theology, but in the rich, symbolic language of the Bible. The liturgy consists largely of long prayers of great beauty and solemnity and of songs and chants set to solemn music and composed for the most part in the golden age of the liturgy between the fifth and the tenth centuries. It is pervaded by a sense of the majesty and the holiness of God, which is typical of the Semitic genius and is found alike in the Bible and the Koran.

There is, in fact, much in common between Syrian Christianity and the Islamic religion which surrounded it and there was at times mutual influence. Thus Bar Hebraeus, one of the great theologians of the Syrian Church, seems to have modelled his mystical treatise, *The Book of the Dove*, on a work of the great Muslim theologian, Al Ghazali. There is in all Semitic religion a profound sense of the infinite holiness of God, his moral righteousness and refusal to tolerate sin, but also of his infinite compassion and willingness to forgive the sinner who repents. There is also in the Syrian liturgy a wonderful sacramental sense; the sense that through the Incarnation the divine power has penetrated the whole creation and man begins to participate in the new life of the Resurrection. This cosmic vision was expressed marvellously in the work of Dionysius the Areopagite, which incorporated so much of Neo-Platonism into Christian theology, and who is now generally believed to have been a Syrian monk.

Yet, though this Syrian Christianity shows the possibility of an Oriental form of Christianity, distinct from all its Occidental forms, it is not enough. It belongs to the Middle East and has affinities with Islam, but it has nothing in common with the Far East or with Chinese and Indian thought. Every form of Semitic religion also has its own serious limitations. Each of them has a deep sense of the holiness of God, of his moral purity and rejection of sin together with his immense compassion and mercy, which represents a profound insight into the nature of Reality itself, yet in each of them there is also a spirit of intolerance, which has become a serious obstacle to their acceptance. Each of them has grown up with the conviction that it alone is the true religion and Christians and Muslims, at least, are driven by the logic of their position to try to convert all others to their faith. When these views are supported, as they have often been in history, by force of arms, the result is disastrous, not only for the religions themselves but also for religion itself.

It is here that the Semitic religions have to learn from the Oriental tradition. In the Oriental religions we find nothing like this. There are innumerable sects and divisions in Hinduism, but though there have been occasional conflicts, they normally manage to live together in peace and harmony, each respecting the faith and worship of the others. In Buddhism also there is the great division between the Hinayana and the Mahayana, the Greater and the Lesser Vehicle, but it has not led to violence and hatred and persecution like similar divisions in the Christian Churches. It is not any particular form of religion, but religion itself which is on trial in the modern world, and only an ecumenical movement among religions, each learning to accept and appreciate the truth and holiness to be found in the other religions, can answer the need of religion today.

I was able to face this challenge of a genuine religious ecumenism, when I moved from Kerala to another ashram in Tamil Nadu, the old Madras State. This ashram was founded by two French fathers, Monchanin and Le Saux, who had been the pioneers in the attempt to adapt monastic life in India to the traditional forms of Indian life and prayer.[4] They called the ashram 'Saccidananda Ashram', *saccidananda* being the Hindu name for the Godhead as Being, Knowledge and Bliss, which they took as a symbol of the Christian Trinity, the Father as Being, the Son, or Word of God, as the Knowledge of the Father, and the Holy Spirit as the Bliss of Love, which unites Father and Son. They themselves took the names of Parama Arubi Ananda, the Bliss of the Supreme Spirit, and Abhishiktananda, the Bliss of Christ. Thus they sought to identify themselves with the Hindu tradition of *Sannyasa*, the renunciation of the world in order to experience the bliss of the divine life. But this was much more than a matter of names. They sought by the study of Yoga and Vedanta to integrate the whole spiritual tradition of India into their lives as Christians, thus working towards that unity of religion which is the goal of mankind.

Unfortunately Father Monchanin died after a few years and Father Le Saux finally settled in the Himalayas as a hermit, where he wrote several books in which he showed the most profound insight into the relation of the Hindu to the Christian tradition. When he left Shantivanam he invited us to take it over and I came there with two other monks from Kurisumala Ashram to continue his work. Here we were able to start our monastic life again in a more radical way. The Benedictine life, to which I had been accustomed, was that of a community of monks sharing a common life, of prayer and study, supporting themselves by the work of their hands. But now I embarked on something different. An ashram is not primarily a community like a monastery. It is a group of disciples gathered round a master, or Guru, who come to share the prayer life, the experience of God, of the Guru. The life, therefore, centres not on the common prayer of the liturgy but on the personal prayer of each member. It is the hour of meditation at dawn and at sunset, the traditional time for meditation in India, which forms the basis of the life, the silent communion with God, and the common prayer of the community is as it were an overflow from this.

In Shantivanam, the Forest of Peace, we each have a small thatched hut among the trees in which we live and pray, and we meet together for prayer three times a day, not for the formal prayer of the liturgy as at Kurisumala, but for a more informal prayer in which there are readings from the scriptures of different religions as well as psalms and readings from the Bible. In the morning we read from the Vedas, at midday from the Koran and the Granth Sahib of the Sikhs, and in the evening from the devotional poets, especially those of Tamil Nadu like the great Tamil mystic, Manikkar Vasagar. We are thus confronted day by day in our prayer with the question of the relationship between the different religions.

It is no longer possible today for one religion to live in isolation from other religions. In almost every country people of different religions and of no religion are meeting with one another and being compelled to face their differences. For a Christian and for members of the other Semitic religions this presents a real problem. Each of them has been taught to regard itself as the one true religion and to reject all other religions as false, so that to enter into dialogue with other religions is not easy. Yet more and more the necessity for contact is being realized, and those who attempt to do so are finding that dialogue, when properly understood, is not a compromise with error but a process of enrichment by which each religion opens itself to the truth to be found in the other religion, and the two parties grow together in the common search for truth. Each religion has to hold the fundamental truth in its own tradition and at the same time to allow that tradition to grow, as it is exposed to other aspects of the truth. Thus we begin to realize that truth is one, but that it has many faces, and each religion is, as it were, a face of the one Truth, which manifests itself under different signs and symbols in the different historical traditions.

The Semitic conception of God is that of an utterly transcendent Being, set over against the world as its Creator and Lord and ruling its destiny from above. The spatial imagery is, of course, only symbolic, but the concept is one of utter transcendence. The Hindu and the Oriental concept of God – or rather of ultimate Reality, since it may not receive the name of God – is that of an immanent power in nature and in man, hidden in the heart of every creature. The figure of Siva Nataraja, the Lord of the Dance, is a perfect symbol of this. He creates, sustains and dissolves the world by his rhythmic dance, and the whole cosmic order is nothing but this dance of Siva. What is distinctive in this vision is that God is conceived not so much above the universe as in it. As it is said in the Upanishads: 'The God who is in the fire, the God who is in the water, the God who has entered into the world, the God who is in the plants and the trees, adoration to that God, adoration to him.'[5]

It is true, of course, that in the Christian tradition God is also conceived as immanent in nature, and St Paul himself quotes the saying: 'In him we live and move and have our being.' But the emphasis is quite different. The Hebrew starts from the transcendence of God and gradually discovers his immanence; the Hindu starts from the immanence and reaches towards his transcendence. It is a difference of point of view. Each is complementary to the other and opens up a different perspective.

When the Christian faith is seen from the Oriental perspective, another aspect of the Truth contained in the original revelation is disclosed. In the first place the use of the word 'God' comes to be questioned. In the context of Semitic thought 'God' is conceived as a Person, but the word 'Person', like all other terms applied to the ultimate Reality, is a term of analogy. This is not to deny personal being in God, but to recognize that he is beyond every concept which we can form and therefore 'beyond personality'. In Christian history, the same perspective was reached by Dionysius the Areopagite who, under the influence of Neo-Platonic thought, described God as 'beyond being'. But for the ordinary Christian brought up on biblical thought, God remains essentially a person and the limitations of such language are scarcely recognized. It seems necessary, therefore, if we are to keep the right perspective to use some phrase like Ultimate Reality, Ultimate Truth or, with Tillich, Ultimate Concern, when speaking of the Godhead itself, as distinct from the personal aspect of God. The Oriental, though using personal language about God, habitually goes beyond such language and speaks of Brahman, Atman, Tao or in the extreme negative language of Buddhism, Nirvana or the Void. These are all words which point towards the nameless reality, which cannot properly be conceived and is as much beyond personality as it is beyond any human concept. But in speaking of God in this way the Oriental is not concerned with theory or doctrine. All Oriental doctrine arises from an experience of God, or Ultimate Reality. In Hinduism Brahman is the name given to that Reality conceived as the Source from which everything comes, the Ground in which everything exists, the Goal to which everything aspires. It is the One, the Eternal, the Infinite, the Transcendent, or whatever name we choose to give to the 'beyond' of human existence.

When the mind in meditation goes beyond images and concepts, beyond reason and will to the ultimate Ground of its consciousness, it experiences itself in this timeless and spaceless unity of Being, and this is expressed in the 'great sayings' of the Upanishads: 'I am Brahman', 'Thou Art That' . . . The Ultimate is experienced in the depth of the soul, in the substance or Centre of its consciousness, as its own Ground or Source, as its very being or Self (*Atman*). This experience of God is summed up in the word *saccidananda*. God, or Ultimate Reality, is experienced as absolute being (*sat*), known in pure consciousness (*cit*), communicating absolute bliss (*ananda*). This was the experience of the seers of the Upanishads as it has been that of innumerable holy men in India ever since. It is an experience of self-transcendence, which gives an intuitive insight into Reality. It is this knowledge which Western man has to learn to acquire. All alike have to discover this other dimension of human consciousness, this feminine, intuitive awareness, in which the rational mind is no longer the master, but has to submit itself to a higher law of its own being and transcend its limitations. This is what the West has to learn from the East and the East has to re-learn, if it is not to lose its own soul.

There are signs already that this new consciousness is beginning to dawn as the West comes into contact with the East. The age of scientific materialism, which dominated the nineteenth century is passing and a new age of spiritual wisdom is coming to birth. Western science itself has prepared the way for this. The 'scientific' image of the world which prevailed from the time of Socrates as an objective reality extended in time and space, which could be observed objectively by a detached human observer, has collapsed under the impact of science itself. The Newtonian universe of solid bodies moving in absolute space and time has given way to the view of relativity and quantum physics.

'In modern Physics,' it has been said, 'the universe is experienced as a dynamic, inseparable whole, which always includes the observer in an essential way.'[6] It is not only that science no longer recognizes a world of separate bodies moving in an objective space and time, but rather a complicated web of relationships between the various parts of a unified whole.[7] It goes far beyond this and recognizes that the human consciousness is essentially involved in the object which it observes. 'Natural Science,' says Heisenberg, 'does not simply describe and explain nature; it is part of the interplay between nature and ourselves.'[8] In other words, science does not give knowledge of reality as such, but of reality reflected through the human consciousness. This, as the author of *The Tao of Physics* observes, brings Western science very near to the traditional Eastern view of reality. There is no objective world outside us as opposed to a subjective world within. There is one Reality, which manifests itself objectively outside us and subjectively within, but which itself is beyond the distinction of subject and object, and is known when the human mind transcends both sense (by which we perceive the 'outside' world) and reason (by which we conceive the mental world of science and philosophy) and discovers the Reality itself, which is both being and consciousness in an indivisible unity.

How, then, are we to describe this new vision of the world, which is also the vision of the ancient seers? We have to say, that there is one Reality, 'One only without a second' which is indivisibly being and consciousness (*sat* and *cit*) and this Reality when known in its origin is experienced as the source of ineffable joy (*ananda*). This one Reality is manifested to our divided consciousness as on the one hand an 'objective' world extended in space and time and obeying apparently mechanical laws, and on the other hand a 'subjective' world of sensations, feelings, images and ideas arising in our consciousness. We find ourselves divided therefore between conscious and unconscious, psychological and physical, mind and matter, or in Hindu terms between Purusha (Spirit, Consciousness) and Prakriti (Nature or the Unconscious). But the more we penetrate into mind or matter, the more we find that they themselves interpenetrate, that they cannot be divided. Mind and matter, conscious and unconscious, Purusha and Prakriti, interpenetrate, and at the deepest level of consciousness the division disappears, mind and matter, Spirit and Nature, are one.

In other words, there are three worlds, the worlds of matter, mind, and Spirit, which we experience in ourselves as body, soul and spirit. But these worlds are not really divided. It is due to ignorance (*avidya*) and illusion (*maya*) in Hindu terms, to sin and the Fall in Christian terms, that we experience this division in ourselves. The aim of all religion is to restore this undivided consciousness and unity of being to man, which in Hinduism is called moksha or liberation, in Buddhism nirvana or 'suchness', and in Christianity is represented by the redemption of man and his restoration to union with God.

Primitive Man experienced this undivided unity of being and consciousness and expressed it in terms of Myth. For

Myth in its origin is the symbolic expression of the one Reality experienced as a living unity in an undivided consciousness. Vedic man, for instance, in whom the mythical consciousness is most richly developed, experienced the world and himself in what Dr Panikkar in an awkward but significant term has called a 'cosmotheandric' unity. In other words, God, man, and the world are originally experienced in a total unity. But as Reason developed distinctions began to be made and the original unity was broken up. It was necessary, of course, for reason to develop and for distinctions to be made. But in the process man has become divided. He experiences himself as divided from nature and from God and divided in himself. This in Christian terms is the Fall of Man. It is a fall from a state of undivided consciousness into a state of divided consciousness. In past times this division was experienced in varying degrees, but in modern times it has reached the furthest limit. Never before has man felt so isolated, alone in a vast, impersonal universe obeying mechanical laws, shut up in his own individual consciousness divided both from nature and from God. But this, of course, is an illusion; this is the great Maya, the ignorance, the Sin, which every religious tradition has seen to be the cause of all human misery. There is no external universe outside us obeying mechanical laws. The whole universe is penetrated by Mind; it obeys, when rightly seen and understood, not merely mathematical laws but the law of the Spirit. 'The Spirit of the Lord has filled the world.'[9] To realize this living unity of man and the world in the life of the Spirit has been the purpose of all ancient religion.

The myths and rituals of primitive peoples, the Australian Aborigines, the African Bushmen, the American Indians, tribal people everywhere, have all been seen as ways to set man free from his isolation and restore him to unity with himself and the universe. In India today this primeval religion is still a living reality, rooted not only in myth and ritual, as conducted daily in the temples, but also in profound philosophical reasoning. In the Upanishads and the subsequent systems of Vedanta the mythical world of the Vedas was submitted to searching philosophical investigation, and we have in the Vedanta the most profound and systematic study of the ultimate nature of Reality to be found in the history of the world.

How, then, does the Bible fit into this pattern of human development? We have to recognize first of all that the Bible belongs essentially to this world of Myth. Myth, as we have said, is the symbolic expression of Reality in terms of the human imagination. The story of Adam and Eve and Paradise is clearly a mythological story of the origin of man and his Fall from his original state of unity with God. The story of the Redemption of Man, the Son of the God becoming man, of his death and resurrection, of his descent into Hell and his ascension into Heaven, of his coming in glory at the end of time, is clearly the language of mythology. This, of course, is not to say that it is not true, but on the contrary that it is the nearest to the Truth that we can come. It is an illusion to think that scientific language is 'true' and poetic language is 'untrue'. Scientific language, above all in its most typical form of mathematics, is the most abstract and unreal language that is, furthest from the total concrete reality. Poetry, or the language of symbolism, is nearer to reality but Truth itself can only be known by a pure intuition which is beyond all language.

The Bible, like all religious literature, is rich in this language of symbolism but the symbolism of the Bible is distinguished by the fact that it is a historical symbolism. History is the record of events, not merely the physical event in space and time, but also the psychological event, the meaning of the physical events in human consciousness. In this respect poetry is often nearer to the reality than bare history. Homer's *Iliad* brings us nearer to the reality of the Trojan War than any history could do, and Tolstoy's *War and Peace* gives an insight into the reality of Napoleon's invasion of Russia which no history could give. But Homer and Tolstoy also give an insight into the cosmic order behind the human story and help us to realize something of the meaning of human history as a whole.

It is to this world of historic symbolism that the Bible belongs. The Bible is history, the record of events in the history of a particular people, which can be situated in the concrete historical circumstances of the time. In the New Testament in particular Jesus is placed in a historic situation, born in the reign of the Emperor Augustus, a contemporary of Virgil and dying 'under Pontius Pilate', the Roman governor of Palestine. But this history is placed in the light of an imaginative vision of human history seen as a progressive movement towards an 'end', an *eschaton*, when the full meaning of human history will be revealed.

There is thus profound psychological as well as historical truth in the Bible, but above all, it is a record of events seen in the light of ultimate Reality. Jesus is seen as the Person in whom the ultimate meaning of human life and history is revealed. This is expressed in the symbolic language of the Hebrew tradition, of the coming of the 'kingdom of God', of the 'Son of Man' who is also 'Son of God', of his birth to a Virgin, of his death and Resurrection and Ascension. This is clearly the language of mythology, that is of symbolism, but it is based on actual phsyical and psychological events. It is no use trying to separate the physical from the psychological so as to arrive at some abstract 'scientific' reality. The physical and psychological events have to be seen in the light of the total Reality and then their true meaning becomes clear. Jesus was man in the sense that he possessed a human body and a human soul like every other man, and he experienced himself through this human body and soul as other men do. But in the depth of his spirit, in that Ground or Centre of the soul, which exists in every man, he knew himself as one with that ultimate Reality, which he called God, and he experienced himself in this Ground of his being in the relationship of a Son to a Father. This experience of relationship, which he expressed in terms of knowing and loving the Father and being known and loved by him, seems to be the unique character of Jesus's experience of God. There is no reason to doubt that Jesus experienced his relationship to God in this way, though the way in which it is expressed in the New Testament, especially in St John's Gospel, is clearly a development of his original teaching.

If we want to translate this symbolic language of the Bible into more universal terms, we can say that the one Reality, God, Truth, Spirit, by whatever name we choose to call it, has been manifesting itself from the beginning in all creation and in all human history and in every human consciousness. But though the one Reality is manifested in the world, it is also hidden. Every man and every thing both hides and reveals the Reality. In certain holy people everywhere the Reality becomes, as it were, transparent. The unity of man and the universe begins to shine through. This vision of Reality is embodied in the myths and rituals, the doctrines and sacraments of the different religions throughout the world. In each religion the divine Reality is manifested under different signs and symbols and we need to be able to discern this hidden Truth in each religious tradition. Each has something to contribute to human understanding and to human fulfilment.

In Christianity the divine Reality manifested itself in the Person of Jesus, in his life and death and resurrection. This was a unique historical revelation within a unique historical tradition, with both its values and its limitations. Jesus came at the end of a long historic process to bring to fulfilment the hopes of a particular people and to reveal the final purpose of God in their history and in human history as a whole. The birth of Jesus from a Virgin was the sign of the birth of a new humanity, born 'not of the will of the flesh, or of the will of man, but of God'.[10] His miracles were the sign of the 'new creation'[11], the transformation of matter by the Spirit, that is, through its penetration by consciousness. His death and resurrection were the sign of the passage through death to new life in the Spirit, which man has to undergo in order to 'realize' God. His 'descent into hell' and his 'ascension into heaven' are the signs of the penetration of the Spirit into the depths of the Unconscious and the passage to the Super-conscious state, the 'fourth' state of Hindu tradition, which is beyond our present state of consciousness in space and time. Finally, his Second Coming is the final manifestation of the Truth, of Reality itself, when the whole creation and the whole of humanity passes out of its present state of being and consciousness into the total consciousness of Reality – the Being, Knowledge and Bliss of Saccidananda.

Jesus, therefore, knew himself in the depth of his consciousness as the New Man, in whom the destiny of mankind is revealed. The sin which brought a divided consciousness into the world is overcome, and nature and man are restored to their original unity with God. In the Resurrection the body and soul of Jesus were transformed by the Spirit and the total Reality of God, man and nature was revealed in its indivisible unity, a unity which is at once physical, psychological and spiritual. But beyond even this Jesus reveals a further depth in the Being of God. Jesus knew himself in the depth of his Spirit beyond time and space as the Son of the Father, participating in the knowledge of God and communicating in his Bliss. Yet this was not a pure identity of Being and Consciousness, but a communion of love. The Father loves the Son and the Son loves the Father and they are united in the love of the Holy Spirit, which is the expression of their mutual love.

This, of course, is 'mythological' language, but it expresses a profound metaphysical truth, the truth that Being itself is not only consciousness but also love, that there is relationship at the heart of Reality. In thus revealing his own relationship to God as his Father in the love of the Spirit, Jesus also reveals what is the destiny of man. Every man is destined to discover this relationship of Sonship in the depth of his Spirit. As we pass beyond our limited rational consciousness and become aware of the depth of the Spirit within, we discover this unfathomable depth of knowledge and love opening up within us and uniting us to one another and to the whole creation in the light of God. And this is not an identity of being without distinction but a communion of love, by which each is 'in' the other, as Jesus expressed it in his high-priestly prayer: 'I in them and thou in me, that they may be perfectly one.'[12]

How then are we to understand the Church in the light of this perspective? The Church in this sense is clearly the communion of those who are united by the love of the Spirit in the knowledge of the Word of God, the Eternal Truth, and through him return to the Father, the Source, the Origin and Ground of all creation. But the Church has also a beginning in time as a historical institution. When the Holy Spirit descended on the disciples at Pentecost, the power of the Spirit which had transformed the body and soul of Christ at the Resurrection was communicated to his disciples. A new consciousness dawned, a consciousness beyond the ordinary rational consciousness, which set the disciples free from the limitations of our present mode of existence and consciousness and opened to them the new world of the Resurrection. The Church is the community of those, who experienced this new birth 'in the Spirit' and whose lives were transformed by the experience. The effect of this was seen in the fact that they were 'all of one heart and mind'[13], and that they sold all that they possessed and 'had everything in common'[14]. The new life in the Spirit thus penetrated the economic and social order and brought a power to transform human society but it remained essentially beyond our present human limitations. The Church was from the beginning a 'charismatic' community, a community of the Spirit.

Yet it had also an elementary organization. Jesus left behind him twelve 'apostles', whom he clearly intended to be the nucleus of the new Israel, a new 'People of God'. There was also a ceremony of initiation into the new life and a meal in common, in which the new life with Christ was shared. This was apparently all that he left by way of organization. In the course of time other ceremonies were added and 'elders' and 'overseers' were appointed in the different Churches, but these seem to have been appointed as the need arose. There was a reason for this. Jesus left his disciples with the expectation that he would return again in their own lifetime and bring about the final 'restoration of all things'. This is the perspective of the New Testament.

Jesus was not concerned with the 'history' of the Church as an institution, but with its transcendent Reality. Jesus himself enjoyed the new life of the Resurrection, and his disciples were called to share this new life with him. The historical development of the Church is secondary to this great reality of the experience of the Spirit in the new life of the Resurrection. In this perspective the time of the second coming is of little importance. As the second letter of Peter was to say, when the time of his coming was questioned: 'A thousand years in his sight are but a day.'[15]

It would seem that the Christian Churches have to recover this perspective, which is that of the New Testament, if they are to recover their meaning in the world today. The Church has its place in human history, but for the Church, as for Christ himself, history is subordinate to the transcendent reality of life in the Spirit. The organization of the Church as a human community is necessary for its evolution in history, but it belongs to this world of signs and appearances, not the world of ultimate Reality. In the course of history the organization of the Church has grown in various ways and its faith has come to be expressed in various creeds and formulas, but these developments are all conditioned by historical circumstances and none of them can be considered as final and definitive.

A Catholic may believe that the development of episcopacy and papacy and the elaboration of the doctrine and sacramental life of the Church in later times has been the work of the Holy Spirit, but he need not deny that other Churches have also been guided by the same Spirit and he will always be conscious that the Church is a living and growing organism so that its discipline and doctrine are always capable of reform and renewal. What remains fundamental to all Christian Churches is a common faith in Jesus Christ as Lord and Saviour, which was expressed in the early Church in the simple formula, 'Jesus is the Lord'[16], and a common baptism by which all alike receive forgiveness of sins through the gift of the Holy Spirit and are made members of the one Body of Christ. This common basis of faith for all Christians was summed up by St Paul in the formula, 'one Lord, one faith, one baptism, one God and Father of all'[17]. This alone is sufficient basis for Christian unity.

But beyond this we have to enlarge our vision of the Church to include not only all Christians but also all those who sincerely seek God. As we have seen, God is revealing himself at all times to all men in all circumstances. There is no limit to the grace of God revealed in Christ. Christ died for all men from the beginning to the end of time, to bring all men to that state of communion with God, with the eternal Truth and Reality, for which they were created. This gift of eternal life is offered in some way to all men without exception. Wherever man encounters God, or Truth, or Reality, or Love, or whatever name we give to the transcendent mystery of existence, even if he is formally an atheist or an agnostic, he encounters the grace of God in Christ. For Christ is the Word of God, the expression of God's saving purpose for all mankind. That Word 'enlightens every man coming into the world'. Everyone either in life or in death is brought into contact with that Word, that Truth, in some form or other and everyone who responds to that Word is a member of that body of redeemed humanity which is the Church. In a broad sense, therefore, we have to say that every human being is potentially a member of the Church. The Church is an open society. These who belong to the visible Church by faith and baptism are not an exclusive group of the 'saved', but a sign or sacrament of salvation, that is to say, they manifest God's saving purpose for all mankind.

But the question remains, are there some who do not attain salvation? The Christian Churches have always maintained that eternal punishment awaits those who reject God. What

are we to say about this? Of course, the language which the
New Testament uses about heaven and hell is mythological
language. Jesus himself spoke of it always in parables, and no
other language can properly be used, since heaven and hell
are names for the ultimate state beyond our present mode of
consciousness. But what is signified by this language? We
must be clear in the first place that the ultimate state is beyond
time and space.

There can therefore be no question of suffering – or of
happiness – going on in an endless time. Eternity is a timeless
moment and a spaceless point. It is total realization of being in
pure consciousness, of absolute bliss. But outside this state
there is ultimately no being at all. Sin and evil, as we know
them, are the effects of a divided consciousness, a consciousness conditioned by space and time. Such a consciousness
cannot be eternal; it belongs essentially to this world of
becoming and of change. Hell can therefore be nothing but
the loss of God, the loss of one's soul, the failure to 'be'.
Ultimately, there is only one Reality, one Being, one eternal
life and Truth. To realize this Truth is eternal life; to fail to
realize this Truth, which is a truth of being, is to fail to be.
There is no being outside God. This, at least, would seem to
be a possible interpretation of the meaning of heaven and
hell, yet when we speak of the ultimate state we are speaking
of a mystery which cannot properly be expressed, and all
language is defective. But at least, we can dismiss from our
minds all thought of an endless suffering in time.

When I and my friends were led to reject the industrial
revolution, and to try to shape our lives by a simpler and
more traditional way of life, we were almost blindly seeking
an escape from the world in which we had grown up and
trying to discover a more natural way of life on our own. But
since that time this rejection of the present system of

civilization has spread throughout the world. Everywhere there is a search for an 'alternative society', a way of life which will be more natural and more human and is equally opposed to the capitalist and the communist systems.

I myself was led to the discovery of religion and Christianity as giving a meaning to life, and to the monastic life as an alternative way of life. Yet it is clear that religion and Christianity, and to a large extent monasticism, are caught up in the present system, and have failed to offer the way of life which people are seeking.

It would seem that we have come very near to the state of the Roman Empire in the fourth century after Christ. At that time there was a flourishing Christianity. The Councils of Nicaea and Constantinople had laid the foundations of Christian doctrine which were to prevail for the next thousand years, and the Church had been organized in a system of government which has survived even to the present day. There were, moreover, great saints and doctors of the Church, who remain as examples of wisdom and holiness, who are still a source of inspiration today. Yet the Roman Empire, and the whole system of civilization based upon it, was unable to survive. By the beginning of the next century the collapse had begun and by the end of the century it was complete. It would seem likely that the same fate awaits the present civilization. By the end of this century the shortage of the natural resources, on which the whole system depends, will have brought about a fundamental change in the present way of life. The search for an alternative form of energy may decide the future of our civilization. If the choice of nuclear energy is made then it may well lead to the destruction of this world, but if an attempt is made to use the natural sources of energy in the sun and water and wind, it may be that civilization will survive.

But whatever the fate of this present world, the real need is to find a way of life which is able to survive all such disasters. In the Roman Empire it was the monastic life which saved the world. It was the monks who fled to the deserts of Egypt, Palestine and Mesopotamia, and founded a way of life based on prayer and work in conditions of the utmost poverty and simplicity, who alone survived the collapse of the Roman Empire, and whose teaching and example led to the foundation of monasteries all over Europe, in which the basis of a new civilization could be found.

Today there has been a revival of monastic life all over the world. Communities are to be found in Asia, Africa, and South America as well as in Europe and North America. Many are too much involved in the present industrial system to offer real hope of an alternative way of life, but many are seeking to adapt themselves to the problems of the Third World. The hope of the future would seem to lie with the small communities, sometimes associated with a larger community, which are springing up all over the world, consisting of men and women, married and single, seeking a new style of life which will be in harmony with nature and with the inner law of the Spirit. These communities cross all barriers of race and religion and are the expression of the urge to go beyond the present economic, political and religious systems and to open a way to the future of man. They can be likened to the monasteries of the Middle Ages, the centres of a ferment which would gradually transform society and make possible a new civilization.

It is to such a community that now at the end of my life the Golden String has led me. It was put into my hands while I was still a boy at school and led me first to the discovery of God, then to the discovery of Christ and the Church. I thought then that I had reached the end of my journey, at least in this world, but then it led me to India, and a whole new understanding of the world opened before me. At every stage I have been conscious that it was not I who was leading, but that something was leading me. Now it has led me to the point where I have become a 'Sannyasi'. A Sannyasi is one who renounces the world to seek for God, but his renunciation goes far beyond what is ordinarily understood by the 'world'. A Sannyasi is one who renounces not only the world in the biblical sense of the world of sin, the world which today is so clearly set on the path of destruction. A Sannyasi renounces the whole world of 'signs', of appearances.

The world which is studied by science, the world of politics and economics, the world of social and cultural life, which most people take for reality, is a world of appearances with no ultimate reality. It is all passing away at every moment and everybody is passing with it. The Church also belongs to this world of 'signs'. The doctrines and sacraments of the Church are human expressions or signs of the divine reality, which are likewise destined to pass away. So also Christ himself is the 'sacrament' of God; he is the sign of God's grace and salvation, of God's presence among men, and this sign also will pass, when the Reality, the thing signified, is revealed. Finally God himself, in so far as he can be named, whether Yahweh or Allah or simply God, is a sign, a name for the ultimate Truth, which cannot be named. Thus the Sannyasi is called to go beyond all religion, beyond every human institution, beyond every scripture and creed, till he comes to that which every religion and scripture and ritual signifies but can never name. In every religion, whether Christian or Hindu or Buddhist or Muslim, it has been recognized that the ultimate Reality cannot be named and the Sannyasi is one who is called to go beyond all religion and seek that ultimate goal.

Yet when we say that the Sannyasi goes beyond religion this does not mean that he rejects any religion. I have not felt called to reject anything that I have learned of God or of Christ or of the Church. To go beyond the sign is not to reject the sign, but to reach the thing signified. In the language of St Thomas Aquinas, it is to pass from the *sacramentum* to the *res*. As long as we remain in this world we need these signs, and the world today cannot survive unless it rediscovers the 'signs' of faith, the 'Myth', the 'Symbol', in which the knowledge of reality is enshrined. But equally fatal is to stop at the sign, to mistake the sign for the ultimate reality. It is this that sets one religion against another and divides Christians from one another, from people of other religions and from the rest of the world. This is essentially idolatry. Whether it is the Bible or the Church or any dogma or creed, when it is forgotten that they belong to the world of signs and appearances, to the world which is passing away, they become idols far more deadly than any graven image. The Sannyasi is one who is called to witness to this Truth of the Reality beyond the signs, to be a sign of that which is beyond signs.

But when we have said this, we have admitted that the Sannyasi, though he may witness to the world beyond signs, yet himself still belongs to this world. To be true to his vocation he also must disappear, as Jesus himself, the great Sannyasi, disappeared after the Resurrection. He showed himself to his disciples after his Resurrection speaking of the kingdom of God[18], and then he disappeared. Only when he had gone could the Spirit come. As he himself said: 'It is for your advantage that I go from you, for if I do not go the Spirit will not come.'[19] Like the Master, the disciple must

43

disappear. 'Unless the grain of wheat die, it cannot bear fruit.'[20] We have to die in order that we may live. An 'Ashram' is only a stopping place, in which a Sannyasi may live for a time – or for all 'time' – but he is always journeying beyond time to the eternal reality. So also every Church, every religion, every human community, is only a stopping place, a tent which is pitched on this earth by pilgrims who are on their way to the City of God.

I had said[21] that the dogmas and sacraments of the Church are the 'walls of Jerusalem', the City of God, and that faith is the gate by which we enter the City. But when we have entered the City there are no more walls and no gates, for faith itself must pass away. The City itself is without boundaries in time or space. In it everything is contained: both heaven and earth, both fire and air, both sun and moon, and whatever there is in this world,[22] but no longer divided by sin and ignorance, no longer limited by space and time, but all realized in the one Reality, which is pure Consciousness, the consciousness of the eternal Logos[23] and unending bliss, the bliss of the Holy Spirit, which is love, peace, joy.[24]

There are many people today who think that the kingdom of God will come in this world, that peace will be established on earth, that mankind will enjoy lasting happiness. But all this is an illusion. It is the great 'maya' which deceives the world which veils the truth. It arises from a refusal to face death. For those who seek fulfilment in this world, death is an end, a boundary that cannot be passed. But for these who are willing to die, death is the gateway to eternal life.

The new world, the world which we seek, is the world of the Resurrection. But this world is already present among us. The kingdom of heaven is in your midst.[25] Death is the breakthrough to a new consciousness, a consciousness which is beyond the senses and beyond the mind and opens on the eternal and the infinite. We may only catch glimpses of it now, but it is spreading throughout the world: 'The former things have passed away. Behold, I make all things new.'[26]

II

The Vedic Revelation

I

THE VEDIC MYTH: THE COSMIC VISION

I have said that since my coming to India I have been led in a strange way to retrace the path of the Golden String. My awakening to the mystery of existence had come to me through the experience of the beauty of nature, which I have described in the opening chapter of *The Golden String*, and this experience had been expressed and interpreted for me in the writings of the Romantic poets, Wordsworth, Shelley and Keats. Wordsworth had taught me to find in nature the presence of a power which pervades both the universe and the mind of man. Shelley had awakened me to the Platonic idea of an eternal world, of which the world we see is a dim reflection. Keats had set before me the values of 'the holiness of the heart's affections and the truth of the imagination'. These were for me not merely abstract ideas but living principles, which were working in me over many years and which I tried to comprehend in a reasoned philosophy of life.

But when I came to India these ideas took on a new life. I discovered that what in Europe had been the inspired intuition of a few poets, had been the common faith of India for countless centuries. That power which pervades the

46

universe and the mind of man had been revealed with marvellous insight in the Vedas centuries before the birth of Christ. The eternal world of Plato was only a reflection in the Western mind of the profound intuition of the seers of the Upanishads. Above all, I found that that 'truth of the imagination', of which Keats had spoken, was a primordial truth, a truth which takes us back to the very roots of human experience. The Western mind from the time of Socrates and Plato had concentrated on the development of abstract, rational thought which had led to the great systems of theology in the Middle Ages and to the achievements of modern science and philosophy. But India had been nourished from the beginning by the truth of the imagination, the primordial truth, which is not abstract but concrete, not logical but symbolic, not rational but intuitive. So it was that I was led to the rediscovery of the truth which the Western world has lost and is now seeking desperately to recover.

The Vedas, which contain the germ of all the later developments of the Hindu genius, probably took their present shape in the second millennium before Christ, but their roots go back to far more ancient times and take us back to the very beginning of human speech. Perhaps nowhere else can one observe the whole process of human evolution from its primordial utterance to the most elaborate poetic speech and the most profound philosophy. The Vedas are known as *sruti*, that which has been 'heard'; they are not merely the product of human ingenuity but of revelation, that is an 'unveiling' of the truth. They are also called *nitya*, that is 'eternal', signifying that they do not derive from this world of time and change, but are reflections of the eternal. Finally, they are said to be *apauruseya*, 'without human authorship', they are expressions of the eternal word, the

Vac, and the human authors are *rishis*, those who have 'seen' the truth, and 'poets' (*kavi*), those whose utterance is inspired. This shows how in ancient times speech – the word – was held to be something divine, a gift of God, and poets, those who had the gift of speech, were inspired by God.

Human speech was originally poetic; as Vico[1] wrote: 'Poetry is the primary activity of the human mind. Man before he has arrived at the stage of forming universals forms imaginary ideas, before he can articulate, he sings, before speaking in prose, he speaks in verse, before using technical terms, he uses metaphors.'

It is difficult for modern man with his prosaic mode of thought to realize that poetry is more natural to man than prose, and yet all the evidence of history shows it. The further we go back in time the more we come not on prose but on poetry. The literature of India begins with the hymns of the Rig Veda, that of Greece with the poems of Homer. The Bible itself is as much poetry as prose, and its earliest strata are all poetic. The reasons for this are obvious. Poetry is the expression of the whole man. It expresses not merely his mind but his sensations, his feelings, his 'heart's affections'. This is why the imagination, as Wordsworth and Coleridge and Keats so well understood, holds the key to human understanding. The imagination is the link between the mind and the heart, between intellect and sense, between thought and feeling. Modern man has broken this link; he has created a world of science and reason, whose language is prose, and has cut himself off from the sources of life in the imagination, which is the language of the heart.

Ancient man, that is man from the earliest times until the first millennium before Christ (and even after that in the greater part of the world until the present day), lived in the world of the imagination, that is the world of integral wholeness. Of this world of the imagination the supreme expression was the Myth.[2] Myth is a symbolic utterance which arises from the depths of the unconscious, or rather from the deep levels of consciousness which lie below the level of rational consciousness. The rational mind, with its abstract concepts and logical constructions, is like the tip of an iceberg, while below it are vast levels of consciousness which link our human nature with the universe around us and with the archetypes or transcendent principles which govern the Universe. The Myth is the reflection in the human imagination of these archetypal ideas, those cosmic principles and powers, which were known in the ancient world as the gods or angels.

Through the Myth ancient man was brought into contact with this world of the gods and of the transcendent Source both of gods and men. At the same time, the Myth took shape in his imagination, engaging all the powers of his being, his intellect and will, his feelings and affections, his senses and his whole physical being. In other words, the Myth was the means of his total integration, with the universe around him, with his own inner experience and with the transcendent world of the spirit.

It may seem an exaggeration to credit primeval man with this exalted consciousness, yet all the evidence of ancient myth and poetry from all over the world confirms the fact of this primitive mode of experience. I myself first received an insight into this when, as an undergraduate, I was lent by C. S. Lewis a book written by his friend Owen Barfield on *Poetic Diction*.[3] I have never looked at this book again but it left an indelible impression on my mind. Barfield showed how a word like 'spirit' (Latin *spiritus*, Greek *pneuma*, Hebrew *ruah*, one may add Sanskrit *atman*) originally had many meanings. It could mean wind or air or breath or life or soul or spirit. A common understanding of this phenomenon is that the word originally meant wind or air, then as the connection between breath and air, and between life and breath and between soul and life was realized, man gradually grew in understanding until he came to conceive of a supreme universal spirit.

Barfield was able to show that this view has no basis in reality. These words, as originally used, contained all these meanings without distinction. That is why primitive language, and the language of the Vedas for instance, is so incredibly rich in meaning. The fact is that in primitive speech a word contains a multiplicity of meanings. The imagination, which is the faculty of primitive thought, expresses itself in symbols (literally, from the Greek, that which is 'thrown together'), which reflect this multiplicity of meaning in a single word. In other words, primitive thought is intuitive; it grasps the whole in all its parts. The rational mind comes later to distinguish all the different aspects of the word and to separate their meanings. These are the two basic faculties of the mind, the intuitive which grasps the whole but does not distinguish the parts, and the rational which distinguishes the parts but cannot grasp the whole. Both these powers are necessary for the functioning of the human mind. Intuition without reason is blind; it is deep and comprehensive but confused and obscure. Reason without intuition is empty and sterile; it constructs logical systems which have no basis in reality.

In the Vedas there is a marvellous meeting of the intuitive and the rational mind. They are deeply rooted in the world of myth, but the rational mind has already begun to draw out all the complex meanings of words and to integrate them in a Cosmic vision. We owe to Sri Aurobindo, the sage of Pondicherry, the understanding of the complex symbolism of the Vedas.[4] For many centuries their deeper meaning had been lost and they had been interpreted with a crude literalism. But Sri Aurobindo was able to show how a deeper psychological meaning underlay the external physical sense. The Vedic seers had reached an understanding of the threefold nature of the world, at once physical, psychological and spiritual. These three worlds were seen to be inter-dependent, every physical reality having a psychological aspect, and both aspects, physical and psychological, being integrated in a spiritual vision. The cows and horses of the Vedas were not merely physical cows and horses, they were also the cows and horses of the mind, that is psychological forces, and beyond that they were symbols of the cosmic powers, manifestations of the Supreme Spirit.

This understanding of the threefold nature of the world underlies not only the Vedas but all ancient thought. In the primitive mind (which is also the natural mind) there is no such thing as a merely physical object. Every material thing has a psychological aspect, a relation to human consciousness, and this in turn is related to the supreme spirit which pervades both the physical world and human consciousness. It is interesting to observe that Western science is now slowly coming round to the Oriental view of the universe, which is, in fact, the view of the 'perennial philosophy', the cosmic vision, which is common to all religious tradition from the most primitive tribal religions to the great world religions, Hinduism, Buddhism, Islam and Christianity.

The view of the universe on which Western science has been built, that of matter as a solid substance extended in space and time, and of the human mind as a detached observer capable of examining and describing the universe and so gaining control over it, has now been demolished by science itself. The Newtonian model of a world of solid bodies moving in space and time has been replaced by the model of relativity and quantum physics, in which matter is seen as a form of energy and the universe as a field of energies, organized in space-time, so as to form a unified and interdependent whole.

This comes very close to the Buddhist view of the 'insubstantiality' (*anatman*) of the universe and of the dynamic character of the elements (*dharmas*) as constantly changing parts of an organized whole. But Western science has been compelled to go even beyond this and to recognize that the human mind as observer is already involved in that which it observes. What we observe is not reality itself, but reality as conditioned by the human mind and senses and the various instruments which it uses to extend the senses. What we observe, as Heisenberg said, is not nature itself but nature exposed to our method of questioning.[5] The old understanding of science is gradually giving way to the view that 'consciousness and physical reality (or empirical reality) should be considered as complementary aspects of reality'.[6]

Thus a revolution is quietly taking place in Western science and it is slowly beginning to rediscover the ancient tradition of wisdom, according to which mind and matter are interdependent and complementary aspects of one reality. The same process can be observed in Western medicine where it is gradually coming to be realized that all disease is psychosomatic and that the human body cannot be properly treated apart from the soul.

We are slowly recovering, therefore, the knowledge which was universal in the ancient world, that there is no such thing as matter apart from mind or consciousness. Consciousness is latent in every particle of matter and the mathematical order which science discovers in the universe is due to the working of this universal consciousness in it. In human nature this latent consciousness begins to come into actual consciousness, and as human consciousness develops it grows more and more conscious of the universal consciousness in which it is grounded. Thus we begin to discover the threefold nature of the Vedic universe. There is the physical aspect of matter (*Prakriti*), the feminine principle, from which everything evolves, and consciousness (*Purusha*) the masculine principle of reason and order in the universe. These correspond to the Yin and Yang of Chinese tradition and the matter and form of Aristotle. Beyond both the Yin and the Yang, beyond both matter and form, is the supreme principle, the ground of Being, the Great Tao, from which everything comes and which pervades all things. In the Vedic tradition the two principles were conceived as heaven and earth, and the whole creation came into being through their marriage.

These two principles, which are to be found in all ancient philosophy, are no less fundamental in Christian doctrine. St Thomas Aquinas, who built up his system of philosophy on the basis of Aristotle, regarded the 'form' and 'matter' of Aristotle as the basic principles of nature. Matter according to this philosophy is pure 'potentiality', form is the principle of actuality. Pure matter, or 'prime matter' as Aristotle calls it, does not actually exist. It is a metaphysical principle which is basic to all physical being. Matter, as we know it, is a combination of form and matter, or of act and potency. In every physical object there is a form, a structure, an organizing power or active energy, and a material principle, a passive energy, a potentiality of being which is actualized by the form.

It is difficult to grasp this principle of potentiality precisely because it has no actuality and is not intelligible in itself; for form is the principle of intelligibility as well as of actuality. It can only be grasped in relation to the form which actualizes it. It can be compared to a womb, a darkness, a capacity of being, to which form brings life and light and actuality. It is the chaos, the 'tohu' and 'bohu' of the book of Genesis. It is the source of flux, of change, of that indeterminacy which science discovers even in the atom. This is what in Hindu tradition is called *maya*, which Sankara described as 'neither being nor not-being'.[7] It is the irrational element in existence, the meaningless, the absurd. Yet this principle is not evil in itself. In itself it is a pure potency, a pure capacity of being, and as such has a kind of purity, an innocence, a simplicity which exists at the heart of creation.

This principle is, of course, not merely a physical but also a psychological principle, since the physical and psychological are but two aspects of one reality. It is the ground of the unconscious in man. Beyond all the levels of human consciousness, mental and imaginative and emotional and physical, there is a ground of unconsciousness, a primeval source, a womb of darkness, from which all life and consciousness springs. It is the world into which we enter in deep sleep, what in Hindu doctrine is called *Sushupti*, the state of being beyond the waking and the dreaming state. It is the source of irrationality, of those violent contradictions in human nature, of the insanity which plagues us. And yet it is not insane or irrational in itself; it is only in association with sanity and reason that it develops these characteristics. In itself, as has been said, it has a certain purity and innocence. It is pure receptivity, which is the feminine aspect of the human soul. The masculine aspect is active and communicative, the feminine aspect is passive and receptive. The feminine has its roots in the unconscious, in the darkness of the womb, and is the source of instability and change like the waxing and waning of the moon; the masculine is the source of stability and order and has its source in the light like the sun. Yet both are necessary for existence – without the feminine principle the infinite variety of nature would not exist; the white light of the sun would never be broken up into the multiple colours of the rainbow.

Moreover, these two principles have their source in the Supreme Spirit itself. The one who is beyond all change and multiplicity manifests itself in these two principles eternally. Purusha is the active principle in the Godhead manifesting itself as light and life and intelligence; Prakriti is the feminine principle, which in the Godhead is the Sakti, the divine power or energy. In the Christian tradition there has been very little recognition of this feminine aspect of God. Yet God is both Father and Mother, and in Oriental tradition this has always been recognized.

It is a fact, however, that in the Bible the name for the spirit (*ruah*) is feminine and in the later Syriac tradition, which preserved the same name, the Holy Spirit was spoken of as Mother. There is also in the Old Testament the tradition of a feminine Wisdom (Hebrew *hochmah*, Greek *Sophia*, Latin *Sapientia*) which reveals a feminine aspect in God. It may be possible therefore to see in the Holy Spirit the feminine aspect of God in the Trinity. The source of the Trinity is both Father and Mother, the Son or Word is the active principle of intelligibility, the source of order in the Universe; the Holy Spirit is the feminine principle of receptivity, an infinite capacity for love, which receives perpetually the outflowing of Love through the Son and returns it to its source in the Father.

The Vedic understanding of the mystery of existence is revealed in the Vedic Myth.[8] This myth centres on the Sun as the source of light. But the Sun in the Vedas is not merely a

55

physical body which gives light to the eyes. It is a cosmic power which gives light also to the mind. The gods (*devas*) of the Vedas are the 'cosmic powers' of St Paul.[9] They are what both the Greek and the Arabian traditions called the 'intelligences' which rule the universe. In the theology of St Thomas Aquinas these are conceived as the angels through whose agency the order of the world is maintained. In the Vedas these 'gods' are all conceived as names and forms (*nama-rupa*) of the 'one being' (*ekam sat*) from which the whole universe, both material and spiritual, derives. The Sun therefore is a god in this sense, the source of intellectual no less than of sensible light. It is to him, under the name of Savitri, that the Gayatri mantra, the most sacred verse in the Vedas, is addressed: 'Let us meditate on the glorious splendour of that divine light (*Savitri*). May he illuminate our meditation.'

In the Vedic myth there is a constant conflict between the light and the darkness. The darkness is represented by Vritra, the primeval monster, who holds back the waters of life and hides the light of the sun. He represents the primeval darkness of the unconscious, conceived as a rocky cavern in which the cows of the sun are concealed. The cows themselves, strange as it may seem to us, are symbols of light. They are called the Cows of the Dawn and represent the rays of the sun, so that the dawn can be described as the releasing of the cows from their pen. But these rays of light are not merely earthly light, they are the light of the mind, and the search of the rishis in the Vedas is a search for illumination of mind. Elsewhere the powers of darkness are called the Panis and their chief is named Vala. It may well be that these sources of darkness represent the dark, Dravidian people who were the enemies of the fair-skinned Aryans, or again they may represent the dark thunder clouds which withhold the rain, but this only reveals the multiple symbolism of the Vedas. Everything has at once a physical and a psychological, including a social, meaning and behind all the symbols is the one supreme Reality which is manifesting itself at every level of existence.

It is this vision of the universe which we need to recover. The Western mind has split the world into two halves, conscious and unconscious, mind and matter, soul and body, and Western philosophy swings between the two extremes of materialism and idealism. This is due to a disease of the mind, a schizophrenia, which has developed in Western man since the Renaissance, when the unitive vision of the Middle Ages was lost. This medieval vision is in other respects no longer adequate, and Western man has to recover his equilibrium by rediscovering the vision of the ancient world, the perennial philosophy, which is fully developed in the Vedanta and Mahayana Buddhism, but is implicit in all ancient religion. In this vision of the world the three principles matter, mind and spirit are seen to interpenetrate one another. It is a disease of the merely rational mind that causes us to see them as separate from one another, to imagine a world extended outside us in space and time, and the mind as something separate from the external world. In reality the world we see is a world which has been penetrated by our consciousness; it is the world as mirrored in the human mind. But beyond both mind and matter there is a still further principle of Spirit which interpenetrates both mind and matter, and is the source of both energy and consciousness.

The understanding of man as body, soul and spirit is found in St Paul[10] and in the early fathers of the Church, though later it was unfortunately displaced by the body-soul conception of Aristotle. But in India this threefold character has always been accepted. Man has a body, a physical organism, a structure of energies, forming part of the physical universe. He has a psychological organism, consisting of appetites, senses, feelings, imagination, reason, and will, which forms his personality and is integrated with the physical organism. But beyond both body and soul, yet integrated with them, is the spirit, the *pneuma* of St Paul, the *atman* of Hindu thought. This spirit in man is the point of his communion with the universal spirit which rules and penetrates the whole universe. This is the point of human self-transcendence, the point at which the finite and the infinite, the temporal and the eternal, the many and the One, meet and touch. It is to this point of the spirit that we are led by meditation, when going beyond both physical and psychological consciousness we experience the depth of our own inner being and discover our affinity with the spirit of God. 'The spirit of God,' as St Paul says, 'bears witness with our spirit that we are children of God.'[11]

Man was created in this state of communion with God, and all ancient religion bears witness to the memory of this blissful state of consciousness. The fall of Man was a fall from this spiritual consciousness with its centre in God to the plane of psychic consciousness with its centre on the ego, the separated human soul bound by the laws of the physical organism. This is the state in which we find ourselves today and for many people even the memory of that higher state of consciousness has been lost. The psychic consciousness dominated by the rational mind is taken to be the norm of human life and as a consequence man finds himself dominated by the powers of the physical world, the 'elemental spirits' of St Paul, or in Indian terms the darkness of ignorance (*avidya*) and the illusion of *maya* which is the world separated from God. In India from the earliest times man has sought to be liberated from this bondage to matter (or *maya*) and to attain to enlightenment, the state of the Buddha, the enlightened one, and so to discover his true self, his spirit or Atman, in which he knows himself as one with God, the universal spirit and source of all.

II

THE REVELATION OF THE UPANISHADS: THE KNOWLEDGE OF THE SELF

The revelation of the Vedas, which was given in the rich poetic language of myth and symbol, was developed in the Upanishads in a more philosophical form. The Upanishads come at the end of the Vedic period (500 BC) and form the basis of the Vedanta – the end (*anta*) of the Vedas. In them is to be found the quintessence of Hindu doctrine, the supreme wisdom, which is one of the great inheritances of mankind. They belong to that period in the middle of the first millennium before Christ, which saw also the rise of Jainism and Buddhism in India, of Taoism and Confucianism in China, of Zoroastrianism in Persia, of philosophy in Greece and of prophecy in Israel. It has been called by Karl Jaspers the 'axial period' in human history. It marked the emergence of rational understanding out of the mythical imagination of the ancient world. From the beginning of history, or more accurately from the time of the first emergence of human speech, man had lived in the world of the imagination, of intuitive wisdom in which sense and feeling, desire and thought and will had all been focused on symbols of words and gestures, of dance and song, of images and paintings, of rituals and sacrifices, in which the world of the gods, of the cosmic and psychic powers, was seen reflected in the human imagination. This was the world of the Vedas. Now in this period of the Upanishads, the rational mind breaks through the image and the symbol and emerges into the light of pure thought. The concept begins to take the place of the image.

Yet we must be clear that this is not a case of reason replacing imagination. It is rather that the 'truth of the imagination', as Keats had called it, emerges into a clearer light. At this period precisely we find the perfect marriage of imagination and reason in intuitive thought. Intuition, as we have said, is at first blind; it is a confused and obscure grasp of reality, in which the seeds of all future knowledge are contained. It is embryonic thought, in which the future structure of thought is contained, as the structure of the mature human being is contained in the embryo. As the power of reason develops, this dark embryonic knowledge, which is the knowledge of childhood, begins to be illumined by reason, and the language of images and symbols is formed, creating the vast, rich world of myth in which man lived for thousands of years. Then in this 'axial' period reason pierced through the veil of the symbol to discover the truth contained in it.

It is impossible to exaggerate the importance of this moment in human history. It is the point at which man reaches the knowledge of himself, the Atman, the Self, of the Vedic seer, the 'know thyself' of the Delphic Oracle. From the night of the moon and the stars with all their brilliance, he emerges into the light of the sun and the day.

But there is no break in continuity at this point. The power of reason which was already at work in the imagination, creating the myth and the symbol, now breaks through into a pure intuition of reality. The first intuition of the soul had been dark and confused, it had grown with the rich symbolic intuition of the imagination; now it passes beyond images and symbols into the pure light of thought. Yet human understanding can never dispense with images and symbols. Even when it passes beyond into pure intuition, it still needs images and symbols to clothe its thought. That is why at this period we come upon the great flowering period of poetry, the epic of Homer and the Greek tragedians, the imaginative genius of the Hebrew prophets, the Book of Poetry in China, the Ramayana and the Mahabharata in India. This is the time when reason and imagination meet in a marvellous marriage, and the masculine and the feminine unite to form the complete man. It is no accident that at the end of this period we meet the figure of the perfect man, in the form of Rama and Krishna in India, the Bodhisattva in Buddhism, and Jesus, the Christ, the Messiah, who brings to fulfilment the promises made to Israel and the prophecies concerning the Messianic Priest and King.

It is to this supreme period in human history, therefore, that the Upanishads belong. They spring from the soil of the rich imaginative tradition of the Vedas, and they bring to it the pure light of the intelligence. At this point we can watch the human spirit emerging into self-consciousness, human reason beginning to form clear concepts and the physical world becoming the object of scientific knowledge. The wisdom of the Upanishads is inexhaustible. It arises from a profound intuition of ultimate reality, a passing beyond all the outward forms of nature and the inner experience of man to the pure intuition of the spirit.

Man is body, soul and spirit. At first the spirit manifests itself in bodily activity, in the search for food and clothing and shelter, in marriage and family life, in religious ritual and sacrifice. But already the powers of the soul, the psyche, are at work, creating language, constructing myths, building up the great world of the imagination. Then as reasoning power develops the spirit begins to manifest itself in rational discourse, in moral perception, in the awakening of self-consciousness. Finally passing beyond the limits of body and soul, man awakes to the reality of the spirit, the transcendent mystery behind all the forms of the universe, behind all human experience, a reality which had been present but hidden from the beginning but now comes into full consciousness.

There are three words which are used to describe this ultimate reality in the Upanishads – Brahman, Atman and Purusha. None of these words is adequate because no words can describe what is ultimate in human existence. As a Buddhist saying has it: 'We use words to go beyond words and reach the wordless essence.' Human language derives from the physical nature of man. 'It was the nerves and not the intellect which created speech,' as Sri Aurobindo has said.[12] Words originally express vital and sensational experience. But this vital and sensational experience gives rise to images which reflect the world in the human imagination. It is then that poetry comes into being. Words are symbols in which the archetypal images of the unconscious are focused and brought into consciousness, so that in becoming conscious of the world around him man becomes conscious of himself. Yet this consciousness is still diffused, the symbol is rich and varied but it is not yet clear. Man is still living in the imagination. The word is accompanied by music and gesture and dance and ritual action. It is the way by which man experiences his oneness with the world. It is only gradually that reason comes in to distinguish clearly the self from the world and the world and the self from their common ground.

The word Brahman is said to derive from the root *brh,*

which means to swell or to grow. This seems to have signified originally the rising of the word from the depths of the unconscious, the growth into consciousness. It is used of the Vedic word or mantra, which Sri Aurobindo has described as the 'voice of the rhythm which has created the world'. Brahman is the mysterious power in nature which comes into consciousness in the word. 'In the beginning,' it is said in the Upanishads, 'this was Brahman, one only.'[13] 'This' is the world, the reality in which we find ourselves, and at this point the intuition is reached that this reality is 'one only'. This is an immensely important stage in human thought when the world in which we live with all its disturbing diversity is seen to be 'one only'. This is the intuition which underlies all Indian thought. It is a fundamental human intuition. In all of us the universe is originally experienced as a unity. As reason develops the different aspects of this unity are discerned, and the underlying unity is very easily lost to sight. This is what has befallen modern man. Reason has grown to such an extent that there is an ever-growing diversity of knowledge, but the unifying vision of the whole is lost in the process. Primitive man had very little knowledge of the diversities of nature, but he had a profound sense of the whole. Everything in nature was related to everything else in a cosmic order. This is the vision of Vedic man. In the Upanishads this principle of unity, this ground of creation, comes into consciousness and is called Brahman.

No words can express what this Brahman is. It is everything and it is nothing. It is the source of all creation, of all the diversities of nature. It pervades all things 'from Brahma (the creator) to a blade of grass'.[14] The whole world, the earth, the water, the air, the sun, the moon, the stars, the gods (the cosmic powers) and their creator, are all 'woven' on this Brahman. He is the 'honey', the subtle essence of everything. In a real sense he is every thing. 'All this (world) is Brahman.'[15] And yet he is nothing: 'he is "not this, not this" (*neti, neti*). There is nothing higher than if one says, he is not this.'[16]

Thus when we come to the ultimate reality, we come upon paradox, and this must necessarily be so. Human reason is a discriminating power. It is the power to distinguish, to analyse, to objectify, that is to make an 'object' distinct from the 'subject'. This is the great divider, which separates man from nature and man from himself. It creates a world of duality and destroys the original paradise in which man had lived in harmony with nature and himself. But when reason has done its work of division and separation it can return to itself, it can re-discover its original unity, it can learn to know the Self.

The Upanishads are the record of this human discovery of the self. They seek to answer the questions: Who am I? Am I this body, this physical organism which is part of the physical organism of the universe, or am I this mind, this soul, which thinks and feels and suffers and enjoys? Or is there something beyond both body and soul, in which the real meaning of my existence is to be found? There is the story of how the gods and demons (the powers of nature both positive and negative) came to Prajapati, the creator, and asked him to tell them about the true self.[17] First he told them to look in a pool of water, so they looked in the water and saw themselves 'even to the very hairs and nails', and thought that this, that is the body, was their self. But then they realized that this was not what they were seeking and so they returned to Prajapati and he told them, 'the self you see in dreams, that is your true self'. So they thought that the inner self, the self of thoughts and feelings and desires was their true self. But then they realized that this was not what they were seeking and so they returned to Prajapati and he said 'the self which exists in deep sleep, when both body and mind are at rest, that is the true self'. So they came to see that the self which is beyond both the body and the mind is the true self, but still they were not content, since that self is unconscious. So they returned to Prajapati again and finally he revealed to them the 'fourth' state (*turiya*), the state beyond waking and dreaming and deep sleep, the state of the awakened self, in which man attains to self-knowledge.

This story is deeply significant. There are three states of consciousness in the Hindu tradition, the waking, the dreaming and the state of deep sleep. Most people think that the real world is to be found in the external world presented to the senses, and that their real self is their bodily existence – the thing which you see in a mirror, the face which you present to the world. When we mature to some extent we begin to realize that the inner self, the self which thinks and feels, with its hopes and fears and joys and anxieties, is the real self. This is what corresponds to the dream state.

But beyond the waking and the dreaming state, there is the state of deep sleep (*sushupti*). This is somewhat surprising from a Western point of view. Most people would feel that the state of deep sleep is simply a state of unconsciousness, and has no significance. But, the Hindu asks, when the body is no longer conscious through its senses, and the mind is no longer conscious through its thoughts, what is that self which remains in deep sleep? It is this self, which is beyond both the body and the soul, beyond all conscious activity, which comes nearest to the real self in the Hindu view. This is the return to the source, to the root, to the ground of being.

But in this state there is no consciousness. It is necessary therefore to go beyond this state to what is called the 'fourth' state (*turiya*). This is the state beyond body and soul, beyond feeling and thought, in which the person awakes to its true being, in which it discovers its ground, its source, not in unconsciousness but in pure consciousness. This is the goal to be sought, in this is to be found self-realization, self-knowledge. This is the knowledge of the Self, the Atman, the Spirit, where the spirit of man reaches and touches the Spirit of God.

We can put it in another way. Human life springs from the darkness of the unconscious, the womb of nature to which we return every night. In that darkness we are one with the earth and the water, the fire and the air. We are in the womb of the Mother. Yet just as all the forms of nature, of sun and moon and stars, of mountains and rivers and seas, are latent in that darkness so all the future forms of life and consciousness are already present in that womb. As the organs of life begin to develop in the child in the womb, so the powers of life begin to develop in nature. The earth brings forth living things, plants and trees and flowers, all these forms were latent in the darkness of the earth, and the light of consciousness, shining in the darkness, brings them forth in the light of day. Life and consciousness are already present in matter from the beginning, but there were no organs through which they could act. In the plant and the tree a dim consciousness is already awakening as recent experiments have proved. They are beginning to emerge from the state of deep sleep, in which the earth is involved, into the dreaming state. The animal lives in the dreaming state. It has appetites, feelings, sensations, imagination, memory and a rudimentary intelligence. The light of consciousness is beginning to dawn, but the animal has no self-consciousness. It remains a part of nature, determined by an external law, reflecting the world, through its senses and ruled by its appetites. In man, nature awakes to self-consciousness. There is a breakthrough from the dreaming to the waking state. Man becomes conscious of himself, conscious of the world, but this also brings with it a relative freedom. He can detach himself from the world around him, from his appetites and desires, and reflect upon himself. That reason which had been latent in matter from the beginning, organizing the stars and atoms, building up the living cell, giving form to plant and animal, now emerges into consciousness. Yet this light of reason is still very precarious. Man is still largely conditioned by his appetites and desires, he still feels himself to be a part of nature, is scarcely conscious of an individual self. Yet that little spark of reason and self-consciousness is there.

It is now that the drama of human existence begins. Man can allow himself to be ruled by his appetites and senses, to submit to the powers of nature and become their slave. Or he can awake to the 'fourth' state, he can discover the source of reason and consciousness within him, open himself to the power of the spirit and awake to his true self. This is what took place in the Upanishads.

All through the Vedic period consciousness had been growing, but it was still an imaginative consciousness. The world was reflected through the human imagination, a world of gods and demons, in which the divine power was mysteriously hidden. But now the mind breaks through into pure intuition of reality. Man's first intuition had been blind and confused, that obscure intuition of ourselves with which we all begin our lives. As the light of reason grew, this intuition had been filled out with the forms of nature, with the consciousness of the world and the self, of physical and psychic being in which the divine spirit was seen to be reflected in the world of gods. Yet the intuition remained of a whole behind all this diversity, of 'one being' (*ekam sat*) of which all the forms of nature and the self were but 'names and forms' (*name rupa*).[18] Now in the Upanishads this intuition issues into the light, into a pure awareness of being, an absolute self-consciousness, an experience of the spirit, the Atman, the self, as the ground of being and consciousness, the source of reason itself.

We must try to fathom this intuition of the Upanishads. It is basic to all human experience, it is the ultimate truth; it is 'that which being known everything is known'. It was discovered by the seers of the Upanishads and has been passed down in India from generation to generation; in it is contained the 'wisdom' of India. It has been known in other religions too, in the traditions of Buddhism and Taoism and in the mystical tradition of Islam. It has been present in Christianity from the beginning, and is the inner secret of the Gospel. But it has often been obscured, and today in the West has almost been lost. It is in the Upanishads that this intuition of ultimate reality has been most clearly expressed and where we can see it, springing, as it were, from its source. But to discover it we have to be able to receive it. It will not yield itself to any merely human effort or learning. 'Not through much learning is this spirit reached, nor through the intellect, nor through sacred teaching, it is reached by him whom it chooses, to him the spirit reveals himself.'[19] This is the great stumbling block. If we think that we can learn the meaning of the Upanishads by any methods of modern science, or philosophy or by Vedic scholarship or linguistic analysis, we are doomed to failure. The Upanishads demand a *metanoia*, a total change of mind, a passage from rational knowledge to intuitive wisdom for which few today are prepared.

Perhaps we can best approach this inner mystery of the Upanishads by way of Katha Upanishad. It is a short

Upanishad belonging to the middle period (about 500 BC), coming after the early period of the long prose Upanishads (the Brihadaranyaka and the Chandogya), written in verse and forming a real initiation into the secret doctrine of the Upanishads. It begins significantly with the descent of the young man, Nachiketas, to the realm of the dead to receive instructions from Yama, the god of death. In every great religious tradition, it has been recognized that to reach the final truth one must pass through death. It is the meaning behind Aeneas's descent into the underworld in Virgil, and of Dante's descent into hell in the *Divine Comedy*. It is, of course, the meaning of Christian baptism. 'You who were baptized were baptized into the death of Christ.'[20] We have to die to this world and to ourselves, if we are to find the truth. What Nachiketas asks of Yama is 'What lies beyond death?' This the question which man has asked from the beginning of history and which people are still asking today. But an answer cannot be given on the level of rational discourse. 'This doctrine is not to be obtained by argument,' says Yama.[21] It can only be learned from one who has had experience of the mystery, who has passed through death into a new life.

This is expressed in the words which take us to the heart of the teaching of the Upanishads. 'The wise man, who by means of meditation on the self, recognizes the Ancient, who is difficult to be seen, who has entered into the dark, who is seated in the cave, who dwells in the abyss, as God, he indeed leaves both joy and sorrow behind.'[22] This is the death we have to undergo, to go beyond the rational understanding, beyond the imagination and the senses, into the primeval darkness, where God, the divine mystery itself, is hidden. It is a return to the womb, to what the Chinese call the 'uncarved Block', to the original darkness from which we came. But now that darkness is filled with light, it is revealed as God. The senses, the imagination and reason by itself cannot pierce through that darkness, but when we die to ourselves, to the limitation of our mind which casts its shadow on the light, then the darkness is revealed as light, the soul discovers itself in the radiance of a pure intuition; it attains to self knowledge.

This brings us to the third aspect of this supreme reality, that of Purusha. Purusha is the cosmic man, of whom it is said 'one fourth of him is here on earth, three quarters are above in heaven'.[23] This is the archetypal man, the pole (*qutb*) or Universal Man, of Muslim tradition, who is akin to the Adam Kadmon, the first man and the son of Man, of Hebrew tradition. This is one of the most profound symbols of the ancient world. It is based on the recognition that man embraces both heaven and earth. Though his body occupies only a little space on a small planet, his mind encompasses the universe. This was beautifully expressed in the Chandogya Upanishad. 'There is this city of Brahman (the human body) and in it there is a small shrine in the form of lotus, and within can be found a small space. This little space within the heart is as great as this vast universe. The heavens and the earth are there, and the sun and the moon and the stars; fire and lightning and wind are there, and all that now is and is not yet – all that is contained within it.'[24] This is based on the view to which we must constantly return, that the universe is a unity and man is a mirror of the universe. He contains within himself the principle of all material elements and of all psychic consciousness, so that he is a 'microcosm', a little world. So it was that the macrocosm, the 'great world', came to be conceived as a Cosmic Man, in whom matter and life of consciousness are gathered into the unity of the spirit.

Purusha is the cosmic person, who contains the whole

creation in himself and also transcends it. He is the spiritual principle, which unites body and soul, matter and conscious intelligence in the unity of a transcendent consciousness. The structure of the universe is described in detail (following the Samkhya Philosophy) in the Katha Upanishad. 'Beyond the senses,' it is said 'are their objects, beyond these is the mind (*manas*), beyond the mind is the intellect (*buddhi*), beyond the intellect is the Great Self (*mahat*), beyond the Great Self is the unmanifest (*avyakta*), beyond the unmanifest is Purusha. Beyond Purusha there is nothing – that is the end, that is the supreme goal.'[25] This is the basic structure of the universe according to the Vedanta. First there are the senses (*indriyas*) and their objects the *bhuta* or elements. Then comes the mind, the *manas*, the discursive mind, which works through the senses, what today is called the scientific mind. It is the lowest level of intelligence, since it is wholly dependent on the senses, and is consequently fragmented and dispersed. Above this is the *buddhi*, the intellect or pure intelligence, the intuitive mind, from which the principles of reason and morality are derived. It is the 'nous' of Aristotle, the *intellectus* of St Thomas, as compared with the *ratio* or reason. It is the point at which the human mind is open to the divine light. It is also the point of unification of the personality. It is at this point that we become fully human. It is at this point that the drama of human existence takes place. If the *buddhi* turns towards the light, it is illumined by the divine light and transmits the light to the *manas* and the senses. But if the *buddhi* is turned away from the light then the mind is darkened and the personality is divided.

Beyond the buddhi is *mahat*, the Great Self, that is the cosmic order or cosmic consciousness. This is a concept which is scarcely to be found in Western philosophy. Yet it is fundamental to the doctrine of the Vedanta. The *buddhi* is the point where the human being is individualized, where man becomes a person. But the human person is not isolated; it is a dynamic point of communion. Just as every element in the physical world is a dynamic point of relationship with every other element, so every human person is a point of intercommunion and the interdependence with every other person. The *mahat* is the sphere of consciousness in which the human mind opens upon the universal mind. In Buddhism it is called the 'store-consciousness' (*Alaya-vignana*). It corresponds with Plato's world of 'ideas'.

Everything in the physical world has a psychic aspect, a psychological character. The idea which was propagated by Descartes, of a material world extended in space and time outside the mind, is an illusion. It corresponds exactly with what in Vedanta is called *maya*. It is a mental fiction. In reality the physical world is permeated by consciousness; it is one aspect of a complex whole. It is like a reflection in matter of conscious intelligence. In the ancient world it was always understood that every material thing has a spiritual counterpart. These are the 'ideas' of Plato, the intelligences of Aristotle and the Arabian Philosophers, the 'angels' of the Greek fathers and the scholastic theologians. These are the gods, the 'devas' of the Vedas.

For modern Western man the gods and angels are relics of a discarded mythology, and of course, they are mythological figures, that is symbolic forms; but they are symbols of realities. They are the 'cosmic powers' of St Paul, the powers that rule the universe – the powers of earth and water and air and fire, of gravitation, magnetism and electricity. But these powers are not outside the sphere of consciousness. Just as our bodies with all their physical and chemical properties are contained within our human consciousness, so all the powers of nature are contained within the universal consciousness, the Mahat. In our experience these powers operate within the sphere of what has been called the Unconscious, but which is really another level of consciousness. Beneath the level of the reflective, rational consciousness there are other levels of consciousness, imaginative, emotional, vital and physical in which the cosmic powers act upon us. The gods and angels are reflections in the human imagination of the 'archetypes', the primordial principles of creation, by which the universe is governed.

These powers, of course, are not only good but also evil. Beside the gods, the devas, are the 'asuras', the demons, and beside the good angels are the evil spirits, the *daimones* of the Gospel. It cannot be too strongly affirmed that these are real powers which act on the unconscious, as depth psychology has recognized, that is, on the lower levels of consciousness, bringing man into subjection to the powers of nature. The fact that modern man does not recognize them is one of the many signs that he is under their power; only when they are recognized can they be overcome.

Yet we must not think of these powers as separate beings without connection with one another. They are all parts of the cosmic whole, in which positive and negative forces are both at work, just as they are in the physical world. They form an ordered hierarchy of being representing different levels of consciousness. In the medieval Christian scheme of the universe there were nine orders of angels, beginning with the angels themselves, who are on a level of consciousness just above that of the rational human consciousness. Above them are the arch-angels, the 'thrones, dominations, virtues, princedoms, powers' of Milton's *Paradise Lost*, the powers at work in the destiny of nations, and finally the cherubim and seraphim, the powers of wisdom and love nearest to the Supreme. The evil angels are powers which are in rebellion against the cosmic order, centres of conflict, of violence and disintegration, at work in nature, in the individual human being and in human society. Of these in the Hebrew tradition Satan is said to be the head, the Diabolos, the Deceiver, the source of the Cosmic illusion, the Maya in Hindu terms, the principle of sin and ignorance (Avidya).

But beyond the Mahat, the Katha Upanishad tells us, is the Avyakta, the unmanifest. This brings us to the two final principles of the cosmic order, in the Samkhya Philosophy, the earliest system of Hindu philosophy, Prakriti and Purusha. The avyakta is Mula-Prakriti, that is Nature, considered as the womb, the Mother, the ground of all the creative powers of the world. Prakriti is the principle of 'potentiality', the first matter of Aristotle, which as we have seen has no being in itself, but is a sheer potency, a *dynamis* in Aristotle's terms, a capacity to be; in this womb of nature the seeds of all future forms of matter and mind lie hid. The gods as well as men all lie hidden in this primal darkness. It is the void, the Emptiness which, in Buddhist terms, contains all fullness. It is the ground of human consciousness, the cave, the abyss of which the Katha Upanishad spoke, the unplumbed depth of consciousness, the deep sleep, from which consciousness arises and the world comes into being. But beyond this avyakta, this Prakriti, is Purusha, the Person, the Supreme, beyond which it is impossible to go.

Purusha is pure consciousness, or rather it is pure being and pure consciousness in one, because at this point all distinction of subject and object disappears. It has been called the 'Person of light consisting of knowledge.[26] But how do we know this person? It is known by meditation. So the Katha Upanishad continues: 'a wise man should keep speech in mind, and keep that in the self which is knowledge. He should keep knowledge in the self which is the Great (the Mahat) and he should keep that within the self which is Peace.'[27] Here we have set before us the path to the knowledge of the Self. We have first of all to enter into silence, to shut out the world of the senses. Then we have to silence the mind, the busy active mind, in the self of knowledge, that is the *buddhi*, the point of integration of the personality. Now we have to surrender this self, the individual self, to the Great Self, the cosmic consciousness, to those higher spheres of consciousness beyond the rational mind.

Then finally we have to surrender this cosmic consciousness, which still belongs to the created world, to the self of Peace, the Peace which passes understanding. At this point we pass beyond the created world, physical and psychological, the world of men and angels, and we enter into communion with the Supreme, the Purusha, the ultimate Reality. Brahman, Atman and Purusha are now known to be one. Brahman is the one eternal Spirit, infinite and transcendent, pervading the whole creation, one and yet manifold, the ground of all creation, 'unseen but seeing, unheard but hearing, unperceived but perceiving, unknown but knowing'.[28] In him all this creation, both gods and men and nature, are contained. Atman is that same eternal Spirit, infinite and transcendent, considered as the self of man, the ground of consciousness. When we transcend the limits of the rational mind and open ourselves to the cosmic, universal consciousness, we are carried beyond the limits of this world, both human and divine, and approach the Supreme, the 'one without a second'. This is the leap of faith, which cannot be reached by any human effort. It is the flight to the One of Plotinus. It is of this that the Katha Upanishad says, 'He whom the Atman chooses, he knows the Atman'.[29] The lower self cannot reach the higher self, it can only allow itself to be drawn up into its presence, to surrender itself to the self, to the spirit within.

This raises the question, What is the relation of the human spirit – the *jivatman* – to the supreme spirit, the Paramatman? Of this the Katha Upanishad says: 'there are the two, drinking their reward in the world of their own works, entered into the secret high place of the heart. Those who know Brahman call them light and shade.'[30] The Svetasvatara Upanishad draws out this image: 'Two birds, inseparable friends, cling to the same tree. One of them eats the sweet fruit, the other looks on without eating.' Then it explains, 'On the same tree man sits grieving, immersed, bewildered by his own impotence (*anisa*), but when he sees the other, the worshipful Lord (*isa*) in his glory, his grief passes away.'[31] This shows clearly the state of the human soul. The soul is set between the physical world, the world of the senses and the world of spirit. When it inclines to the material world and becomes attached to it, it becomes confused and powerless, but when it 'looks up and sees the Lord' then its grief passes away. If we would understand this relationship between the soul (the *jivatman*) and the spirit, we can think of the soul as a glass which is held up to the light of the spirit. When the glass is clouded by sin and ignorance, then the light cannot shine through, but when the glass is clean, then the soul is illuminated by the divine light and the whole being, body and soul, is irradiated by the divine presence.

The spirit in man is the 'fine point of the soul', as St Francis of Sales called it, the point of contact between the human and the divine. It is a reflection of the divine light in us. It is a dynamic point, turned to both God and the world. This is the 'pneuma', the 'spirit' of St Paul, as compared with the 'psyche', the soul, of which he says, 'we have received not the spirit of the world but the spirit which is from God, that we might understand the gifts bestowed on us by God'[32] The spirit in man is a 'gift' or grace; it is the presence in us of the divine spirit. When body and soul are moved by the spirit, then the whole being of man is transfigured. This was the very purpose of creation from the beginning, that body and soul, matter and mind, man and the universe, might be moved by the spirit and drawn into the divine light and life. Sin is the fall from this state of grace into the state of the 'natural' man, the 'anthropos psychikos' of St Paul as opposed to the 'anthropos pneumatikos', 'the spiritual man'.[33]

There are schools of Hindu thought which consider that when the spirit of man (the *jivatman*) is thus united with the spirit of God (the *paramatman*), the individuality is lost. But this is not necessarily so. It is true that the individual soul ceases to exist as a separate being. It is transfigured by the light and participates in the very being and consciousness of God. This is the state of *saccidananda*, the state of being (*sat*) in pure consciousness (*cit*), in which is found absolute bliss (*ananda*). But the soul that enters into this state of bliss does not lose its individual being. It participates in the state of universal being and consciousness, it enjoys perfect bliss, but that personal being which was conferred on it by creation, that unique mode of participation in the divine being, which constitutes it as a person, is eternal. It may be that in the state of union, as many mystics have testified, the soul no longer experiences any difference between itself and God, but the difference remains. The very purpose of creation was that other beings, both men and angels, and through them the whole creation, should participate each in its own unique way in the one being of God. The state of union is often illustrated by saying that it is like a drop of water merging in the ocean, but it can equally be said that it is like the ocean being present in the drop. In the ultimate reality, the whole is present in every part and every part participates in the being of the whole.

This state of union has been beautifully described in the Svetasvatara Upanishad: 'as a metal disk (or mirror) which was tarnished by dust shines brightly when it has been cleaned, so the embodied being (the *dehi* – the dweller in the body) becoming one, attains the goal and is freed from sorrow.' Then the final state of the soul is described in unforgettable words: 'When by means of the real nature of the self he sees as by a lamp the real nature of Brahman, then having known the unborn, eternal God, who is beyond all natures, he is freed from all bondage.'[34] This is perhaps the clearest statement in the Upanishads of the the nature of ultimate reality. It can be known only by the purified self, the spirit in man, cleansed from all attachment to body or to soul. Then this purified spirit sees the real nature of Brahman, the eternal being, mirrored in itself and in the whole creation. Finally this Brahman and this Atman is recognized as the 'unborn eternal God', the personal God, the Purusha, who is the Lord of Creation, beyond all created being.

III

THE REVELATION OF THE PERSONAL GOD

In the early Upanishads, the centre of interest is the Brahman and the Atman, the eternal spirit immanent in nature and in man. Yet this spirit is recognized as also transcendent. It exists in all things, but it also exists without. In the later Upanishads, such as Svetasvatara (c. 300 BC) the transcendent aspect of the one reality comes into evidence. Even in the earliest Upanishad, the Brihadranyaka, we find evidence of this, when it is said, 'If a man clearly beholds this Self as God and as the Lord of what is and what will be, then he is more afraid'.[35] Again in the Isa Upanishad, it is said 'all this, whatsoever moves on earth, is enveloped by the Lord'.[36]

But it is in the Svetasvatara Upanishad that the concept of the personal God is fully developed. There it is said that in the supreme Brahman there is a triad. This triad consists of first of all the *pradhana*, the perishable, that is, the material world: then there are the souls, the *jivatmas*, and finally there is Hara, the Lord, the Imperishable who rules both matter and souls. When a man finds out these three, it is said, that is Brahman.[37] How are we to understand this? What is the relation between God and nature and man, and how are they related to Brahman? There are different schools of Hindu thought in regard to this – *advaita, visistadvaita* and *dvaita*[38] – and the debate continues to the present day. In a sense, of course, there can be no answer to this question. The ultimate reality, whether we call it Brahman or Atman or God, is beyond conception. These are words taken from common speech which reflect the reality but can never express it. This applies to all human speech. Language reflects the world, reality itself, through the medium of the human senses and imagination and the concepts of the rational mind. But the reality itself is always beyond our images and concepts. It can only be known when we transcend both body and soul and experience the one reality in the depths of our being where we are one with that which we contemplate, when being and knowing are one. Yet in the light of this inner experience words can be used to indicate the nature of this reality, words which reflect it, however remotely, and point towards it. This is what we find in the Upanishads.

Let us return to the analogy of the three worlds. There is the material world, including the human body, which is experienced through the senses. But this world, as we have seen, is not independent of the senses. The material world is present to us in and through our senses. This material world, as modern physics describes it, is a field of energies, and our own bodies with their senses and their appetites and their mental images and concepts are part of this field of energies. The energies, which make up the world as we experience it, are both physical and psychological. Together they form an interdependent whole. This is what in Hindu terms is called *prakriti* or nature. But beyond *prakriti* there is *Pvrusha*, the principle of consciousness. Human consciousness is normally reflected through the senses and the imagination, but there is a sphere of consciousness beyond the senses and the imagination, which can be experienced in meditation, in which, as we have seen, the soul attains to self-knowledge by a pure reflection on itself. This sphere of consciousness is *Purusha*, the spirit, the self, which is the source of all consciousness, the principle of all real knowledge, the ground of personal being. In this ground of truth and reality, the source of personal being, all souls find their centre of unity.

Just as the physical and psychological worlds are recognized as an interdependent whole, so in this world of the spirit all consciousness is seen to have its source in one consciousness, an all-pervading spirit, which penetrates and embraces the whole field of physical and psychic energies and unites them in one. This sphere of consciousness can be experienced as the 'ground' of all being, pervading the whole creation, when it is known as Brahman. Or it can be experienced as the ground of human consciousness, the inner spirit, when it is known as Atman, the self, that is the immanent principle of both being and knowing. But it can also be experienced as transcendent being, as 'God' the 'Lord', and then it is known as *Purusha*. This is how the concept of the personal god arises.

Reality is experienced as one, infinite, eternal being, at

once immanent and transcendent, pervading everything and enveloping everything. But this same reality is also experienced as consciousness (*cit*), as a pure intelligence, as totally transparent to itself. But a being possessed by conscious intelligence is what is meant by a person (*purusha*) and so the infinite, eternal spirit, the 'one without a second', is recognized as a person. This is what we find in the Svetasvatara Upanishad. This is a comparatively late Upanishad which marks the awakening of devotion to a personal God. The gods of the Vedas, it is true, were personal, but there each God – Agni, Mitra, Surya – is seen as an aspect of the 'one being' (*ekam sat*), and the ultimate reality itself is not conceived as a personal god. But now in the Svetasvatara Upanishad that step is taken. The ultimate reality, the Brahman, is conceived as a personal being, the object of worship and adoration. So it is said, 'those who know beyond this (world) the Supreme Brahman, the great, hidden in all creatures and alone enveloping everything as the Lord (*Isa*), they become immortal'.[39] This Lord who is one with the Supreme Brahman is said to be the person (*Purusha*) who fills the whole universe. He is called Bhagavan, the name which is universally used of the personal God in India today, and is named Siva.[40]

This name of Siva is of great interest. In this Upanishad, he is identified with Rudra, the God of storm and thunder of the Vedas, who dwells in the mountains. But it seems that he really goes back beyond the Vedas and was originally a Dravidian God. There is a figure found at Mahanjadaro, the ancient Indian city destroyed by the Aryan invaders, which is seated in lotus posture and seems to represent Siva as *Pasupati*, the Lord of creatures. Siva would then have been one of the gods of the indigenous people, an enemy of the Aryans. He is represented as an outcast, dwelling in the graveyard, covered with ashes, as the destroyer, wearing snakes about him and accompanied by demons. He is also the God of fertility, having as his emblem the *lingam*, the male organ, which is represented in the inner sanctuary (the *garbha-griha* or 'womb-house', the source of life) in temples of Siva all over India today.

But Siva is also the great ascetic, dwelling on Mount Kailas, absorbed in meditation, and as destroyer he is conceived as the destroyer of sin who renews the world by his grace. Finally, he comes to be revered as the God of love, his name Siva meaning the 'kindly', the 'gracious', and in a famous Tamil Poem, the *Tirumandiram*, it is said: 'the ignorant think that Siva and Love (*anbu*) are two; they do not know that Siva is love.'[41]

This is a marvellous example of the evolution of a myth. A myth is a symbolic story in which many elements may combine, elements derived from the world of nature and of human psychology, from history and social and economic conditions. In the course of time these different and often conflicting elements are re-interpreted and given new meanings, until eventually a coherent symbol of spiritual reality is evolved. Thus the God Siva for a Hindu devotee today is a name for the ultimate reality beyond name and form, who is one with the Brahman, the absolute truth and the final good, revealing himself to his devotees as a God of infinite grace and love, and the *lingam* is the sign of the formless deity, God beyond name and form.

In the Svetasvatara Upanishad, we can watch this process of the transformation of an ancient myth into a profound philosophical symbol, still retaining its 'numinous' character but developed into a theological figure as the personal god. The God of the Svetasvatara Upanishad is the great Brahman, who is immanent in all creation, but he is also the transdendent Lord (*Isa*) who creates and rules the world by his power. He is said to have his hands and feet, his eyes and ears and head in every place, but at the same time, 'he grasps without hands, hastens without feet, sees without eyes, hears without ears'.[42] He is the *Purusha*, the cosmic person with a thousand heads, a thousand eyes, a thousand feet, but he also dwells within the heart of every creature and encompasses the world on every side. He 'possesses the purest power of reaching everywhere and is the imperishable light'.[43] He is smaller than the smallest, 'the person not larger than a thumb'.[44] Yet he is the creator of all, the great Self, always dwelling in the heart of man, the lord of immortality. Finally, he is the 'lord of lords, the god of gods, the master of masters',[45] the one God of whom there is no place for a second. It would be difficult to find a more impressive expression of the one supreme creator God.

Yet this transcendent God, who creates and rules and encompasses everything, is also said to be immanent in everything and to 'assume all forms'.[46] He can even be said in a sense to 'become' all things. He is the *dehi*, the dweller in body (*deha*), the 'incarnate self', who assumes various forms in various places. Yet at the same time, he has 'no beginning and no end'; he has many forms yet he envelops everything. How are we to understand this? We must go back to the concept of the spirit, the Atman, who is pure being and pure consciousness. It is he who pervades the whole creation, as the active power of energy, life and consciousness in nature and in man. It is he who gives 'form' to every created thing. But he does not merely 'give' form. He is the active principle of form in everything and is present in every particle of matter. St Thomas Aquinas asks in what sense can God be said to be 'in' all things – and he replies that he is 'in' all things by his power, his presence and his essence.[47] By his power, because it is his power alone which gives existence to each thing and preserves it in existence. By his presence, because this power is not exercised at a distance since there is no distance in God, so that he is actually present in every created being. By his essence, because he is not present in part, since there is no part in God, but the very essence of God, in Christian terms, the Holy Trinity, is present in every particle of matter. The divine being, which is also intelligence and consciousness, is therefore present totally in every created thing. It is in this sense that St Paul can say: 'in him we live and move and have our being.'[48]

Can we now see how God, the Supreme Spirit, which is *saccidananda*-being, consciousness and bliss, can be said to 'become' the whole creation? The whole creation exists eternally in God; when God, the infinite being, expresses himself, manifests himself, speaks his word, the whole creation comes into being in that one word. God does not create in time. Creation is an eternal act in God; it is the act by which God himself exists. As Eckhart says, God only speaks one Word, and in that word the whole creation is contained. In God the whole Creation exists eternally in identity with him. As St Thomas again says, the 'ideas' in God, the archetypal forms, which are the principles of all created beings, exist eternally in God and are identical with the divine essence itself.[49] In God you and I and everyone and everything exist eternally in identity with him. This is our eternal archetypal being. When creation comes into being in time, then each of us assumes his own particular created form, his separate identity, but the divine archetype is present still in each one of us. In this sense the world can be said to be a 'manifestation' of God. It is like a mirror which is held up to the face of God. The created world is a 'reflection' of the uncreated archetypal world. Like an image in a mirror, it has only a relative existence. Its existence is constituted by this relation to God. It is in this sense that we can say with the Hindu school of Advaita, that God and the world are 'not two' (*advaita*). The created world adds nothing to God and takes nothing from him. Creation makes no change in him; change is in the creature.

This conception of the world as a reflection, an image, of God is entirely acceptable from a Christian point of view. According to the biblical tradition, man is an image of God, and the Greek fathers interpreted this in the sense that man (and with him the whole creation) is like a mirror held up to the light of God. Each human soul is a reflection of that uncreated light. This is the point of the 'spirit' in man; the point where the human being receives the imprint of the Spirit of God. This again is a dynamic point, a point of receptivity, by which we can either open ourselves to the divine light and grow as persons in truth, or turn upon ourselves and become self-centred, obscured by ignorance and sin. The spirit in man is the point of meeting between God and man, of created being with the uncreated light. In every man the uncreated light is always present – this is his eternal, archetypal being – but whether he receives that light into his soul and is transformed by it, or whether he turns away from the light and becomes darkened and obscured, depends on the inner dynamism of the intellect and will, the created spirit in man. In this sense, therefore, we can speak of God taking the 'form' of man.

The uncreated being, which is pure consciousness and bliss, dwells in the heart of every man, shaping both his body and his soul. While remaining ever the same in his pure consciousness and bliss, he enters into the consciousness of man, into the life of plants, into the energies of matter. He is present everywhere in everything, shaping the forms of matter and life and mind, but remaining in himself ever the same.

This concept of a personal God was further developed in the Bhagavad Gita, which was probably composed at about the same time as the Svetasvatara Upanishad. The Bhagavad Gita forms part of the great epic of the Mahabharata, in which Vishnu rather than Siva is represented as the figure of the supreme God, especially in his 'incarnation' as Krishna. Krishna with Siva is a beautiful example of the evolution of a symbol of God. Unlike Siva, who is essentially a cosmic figure, Krishna seems to have had a basis in history. The Mahabharata itself is the story of a great war, which, like the Trojan War of Homer, must have had a historical origin. But the historical character of Krishna was soon enriched by legend and gradually the figure of a Supreme God emerged, who was like Siva a God of love, and in the Bhagavad Gita is represented as the one Supreme Lord, the creator of all. Nowhere is the utter transcendence of the creator God so clearly expressed as when Krishna says, 'By me whose form is unmanifest, all this world is pervaded; all beings abide in me, but I do not rest in them'. And then lest it should appear that he depends in some way on the world, he continues: 'Yet they do not abide in me; behold my sovereign power! I am the support of all beings but I abide not in them, myself being their cause'.[50]

It would be a mistake to say, as is done in some schools of Hindu thought, that this personal creator God is inferior to the Supreme. Again and again it is shown that Krishna as God is identical with Brahman and Atman. Thus it is said that 'he who knows Brahman (Brahmavid) abides in Brahman (or 'is established in Brahman' – *Brahmani sthita*), his reason (*buddhi*) steady, his delusion gone.'[51] And again: 'He whose spirit (*atman*) is unattached to things without and who finds joy in the spirit having his spirit joined by Yoga to Brahman, enjoys imperishable happiness.'[52] And then a little later, Krishna identifies himself with this Brahman, this Atman. 'He who knows me, who accept sacrifice, and self-discipline, the great Lord of all worlds, and the friend of all beings, attains peace.'[53] Surely it is clear that Brahman, Atman and the 'Great Lord' (*Mahesvara*) are one and the same. They are three names for the same one reality looked at from a different point of view. What the Gita establishes beyond doubt is that that which is known in the Upanishads as Brahman and Atman is also Purusha, the personal God. This is made very clear when it is said: 'There are two spirits (*Purushas*) in this universe, the perishable, and the imperishable' – that is, the world of matter and the world of mind. 'But there is another Supreme spirit (*Purusha*) who is the highest self (*Paramatman*), the changeless Lord, who enters and supports the three worlds.'[54] Here we can see clearly once again the structure of the three worlds – the world of matter, the perishable; the world of mind, or consciousness, the imperishable; and above them both the world of Spirit which pervades the three worlds and manifests himself in all, and hence the words *Brahman, Atman* and *Purusha* can all be used on occasion of each of the three worlds. But the spirit himself is beyond both mind and matter, beyond the perishable and the imperishable, and is therefore known as *Parabrahman, Paramatman, Purushottaman* – the supreme Brahman, the Supreme Self, the Supreme Person.

IV

THE DOCTRINE OF NON-DUALITY

These explanations are necessary, because it is often said that the doctrine of the Vedanta is 'monist' or 'pantheist' or 'polytheist', but none of these terms (all of which are of Greek and not of Indian origin) is accurate. There are monist and pantheist and polytheistic interpretations of the Veda, but the Vedic doctrine itself, the doctrine of the Vedas, the Upanishads and the Bhagavad Gita, is none of these things. It is a doctrine of supreme wisdom, coming down from remote antiquity in the form of a divine revelation, expressed originally in myth and symbol, and developed through profound meditation, so as to give a unique insight into ultimate reality, that is, the ultimate nature of man and the universe.

Though it has come down to us through the Hindu tradition, it belongs not only to India but to all mankind. In fact, there is evidence that this tradition has been known from the earliest times. It is found among primitive people in Africa, Australia, Asia and America, who have received it as an inheritance from their ancestors and have preserved it in their myths and symbols, their rites and ceremonies, their dance and song. It has been called the Cosmic Revelation, the revelation of ultimate Truth, given to all mankind through the Cosmos, that is, through the creation. Of this St Paul says: 'Ever since the creation of the world his invisible nature, namely his eternal power and divinity has been clearly perceived in the things that are made.'[55] In the Hebrew tradition it is preserved in the story of the Covenant with Noah, who is represented as the Father of all mankind.

From the beginning of history, as far as one can tell, man has recognized behind all the phenomena of nature and consciousness a hidden power. Or rather, the phenomena of nature and his own consciousness were all seen to be 'enveloped' in a cosmic whole. As his power of discrimination developed, he was able to distinguish the powers of nature, of earth and sky, of water and fire, the powers of the 'gods', from his own powers of speech and action, of thinking and feeling, and to know himself as a conscious being. But the sense of the whole remained, the consciousness that the gods of earth and sky were also in his heart and mind, and that in myth and ritual, in prayer and sacrifice, he could experience his oneness with the whole creation.

It is this sense of a cosmic unity which lies behind the Vedic tradition, and in the Upanishads the source of this cosmic unity receives a name. It is called Brahman and Atman, and gradually through deep meditation the nature of this Brahman and this Atman was revealed. It is known not by argument or reasoning, not by any activity of the sense or the rational mind, but by an immediate experience of the spirit, the Atman, in man. It is this experience of the spirit which the Upanishads seek to communicate and to interpret in words, as far as it can be expressed in words. It is known as *Saccidananda*, Being or Reality, experienced in pure consciousness, communicating perfect bliss. But such a state of conscious being is a state of personal consciousness. It is misleading to speak of Brahman or Atman as 'impersonal'. A person is a conscious being, a being possessing itself in conscious awareness, and Brahman is therefore the supreme Person, the *Purushottaman*. Every human being is a person just in so far as he participates in this supreme consciousness.

Each of us is conscious in so far as we share in this universal consciousness. The new-born child has a spark of this consciousness in it, which grows as it learns to share through language and gesture in the consciousness of its mother and father, its family and environment. Growth in consciousness is growth in this shared experience of the family, the tribe, the nation, the race. But this consciousness can grow beyond the boundaries of time and space, and enter into a transcendent consciousness, a consciousness transcending the limits of matter and mind, of the categories of sense and reason, and become aware of the universal consciousness which embraces the whole creation. This is the sole source of consciousness in man and the universe. 'There is no other seer but he,' says the Upanishad, 'no other hearer but he, no other perceiver but he, no other knower but he, this Self, the Ruler within, the immortal'.[56] All our seeing, and hearing and perceiving and knowing, is an effect of and a participation in the consciousness of that one, universal Being.

What characterizes this consciousness in the Vedic tradition is its non-duality. Of this it is said: 'Where there is duality, one smells another, one sees another, one hears another, one speaks to another, one perceives another, one knows another, but when everything has become the Self, by what and whom should one smell and see and hear and speak to and perceive and know another? By what should one know that by which all this is known? How should one know the knower?'[57] This is the classical statement of the doctrine of non-duality (*advaita*) and it takes us to the heart of the problem. How should one know the knower? The rational mind can only work through the senses and discover an 'object' of thought. Even the most abstract thought is conditioned by this distinction between subject and object. But how can we know the subject, the I, without turning it into an object? The moment I speak of myself, of an I, I have turned it into an object. This is the limitation of the rational mind. It remains imprisoned in the categories of an objective world. How to escape from the prison of the rational mind?

In all religious traditions, Hindu, Buddhist, Muslim, and Christian, it has been recognized that there is a knowledge above reason, a knowledge which is not derived from the senses and is not determined by the categories of rational thought. It is a knowledge not of an object but of the subject, the I which knows, not the I which is known. In Hindu tradition this has always been regarded as the ultimate form of knowledge, the knowledge of the Self. It must be recognized that this is not a theory which would be a product of the rational mind, but an experience. The mind, turning back on itself, knows itself intuitively. It is an experience in which being and knowing are one – that is why it is called *saccidananda*, because being (*sat*) is experienced in a pure act of knowing (*cit*) in the bliss (*ananda*) of oneness, of non-duality. The knower, the known and the act of knowing are all one. Yet when we have said this, we have already begun to interpret the experience by means of rational categories, while the experience itself is beyond reason. Yet the attempt has to be made, because this experience has often been misinterpreted. It has often been interpreted to mean that the knowledge derived from sense and reason is an illusion (*maya*), and that the world of ordinary experience is therefore unreal. But this is not so. The knowledge of sense and reason itself derives from this universal consciousness. It is the one being who sees and hears and knows in us. Every particular form of human consciousness is a reflection of the one consciousness.

How, then, shall we describe this knowledge of non-duality, this knowledge of the Self? We must say that the one Self, the universal consciousness, is present in all our experience, but its action is limited by the faculties of sense and reason. What we experience is the one reality, reflected through the senses and the rational mind. But when in meditation we transcend the categories of space and time and of the rational mind, we experience this one reality in itself. The finite, changing temporal world of our experience is known in its infinite, changeless ground. All the multiplicity of creation is known in the simple unity of its origin.

But we must not suppose that the multiplicity and variety of the world is lost in this vision of the unity, as though it had no ultimate reality. On the contrary, as has been said: 'Everything that is here is there, and everything that is there is here.' There is not a particle of matter in the universe, not a grain of sand, a leaf, a flower, not a single animal or human being, which has not its eternal being in that One, and which is not known in the unitive vision of the One. What we see is the reflection of all the beauty of creation through the mirror of our senses and our imagination, extended in space and time. But there in the vision of the One all the multiplicity of creation is contained, not in the imperfection of its becoming but in the unity of its being. Of this the great Sankaracharya, the doctor of advaita Vedanta, has said: 'The knower of Brahman enjoys all desires, all delights procurable by delightful objects without exception. Does he enjoy all desirable things alternately as we do? No, he enjoys all desirable things simultaneously, as amassed together in a single moment, through a single perception, which is eternal . . . which is non-different from the essence of Brahman, which we have described as truth, knowledge, infinity (*satyam, jnanam, anantam*).'[58] It is a defect of our minds that we have to go from point to point, from one thing to another, in an ever-changing world. If we had perfect knowledge, we should know the whole in all its parts and all the changing phenomena of nature in an unchanging vision of perfect unity.

But the question remains, What becomes of the individual self in this knowledge of the one Self? Does it simply disappear? Here again it is easy to misinterpret the experience of non-duality. There is no doubt that the individual loses all sense of separation from the One and experiences a total unity, but that does not mean that the individual no longer exists. Just as every element in nature is a unique reflection of the one Reality, so every human being is a unique centre of consciousness in the universal consciousness. Just as no element in nature is lost in the ultimate reality, so no individual centre of consciousness loses its unique character. It participates in the universal consciousness; it knows itself in the unity of the one Being; it discovers itself as a person in the one Person. A person is not a closed but an open centre of consciousness. It is relationship. Every person grows as he opens himself to the totality of personal being, which is found in the supreme Person, the *Purushottaman*. This is what is found in the Christian doctrine of the mystical Body of Christ. This Body embraces all humanity in the unity of the One Person of Christ, and in the final state, as St Augustine says, there is only 'one Christ, loving himself.'[59]

This opening of the individual consciousness on the universal consciousness is a movement of self-transcendence. Every growth in human consciousness is a movement of self-transcendence. The individual self grows by contact with other selves, transcending the limits of its own consciousness by contact with another form of consciousness. Human nature, it has been said, is constituted by its capacity for self-transcendence.[60] The final stage in human growth is reached when the human consciousness goes beyond its natural limits, beyond the categories of time and space, and encounters the supreme consciousness, the consciousness of the One. This is what is described in religious language as 'grace'. As it was said in the Katha Upanishad: 'He whom the Atman chooses, he knows the Atman'.[61] The Atman is the Supreme consciousness, the one Self which is the source of all consciousness in man and in animal. In the human consciousness there is an innate capacity for freedom, the power to choose according to the dictates of reason. When the human consciousness, working through sense and reason, reaches the limit of its capacity, it is drawn by 'grace', by the power of the Spirit, the supreme consciousness working in it, to transcend its personal limitations and to participate in the divine consciousness, the consciousness of the supreme Self. This is what in Hindu tradition is called the 'fourth' state, the state beyond the physical, the vital and the mental, the passing beyond into the state of *ananda*, of bliss consciousness.[62]

V

THE SUPREME SECRET

At this point the Gita introduces another aspect of the divine nature – the dynamism of love. The culmination of the revelation of Gita is the revelation of divine love. 'I am supremely dear to the wise,' says Krishna, 'and he is dear to me.' So far we have seen that man can love God and find supreme happiness in that love or devotion (*bhakti*). But now it is seen that God returns that love. This comes to a head in the last book of the Gita where Krishna speaks his 'supreme word', the 'most secret' of all, when he says, 'Give me thy mind, give me thy heart and thy sacrifice, and thy adoration. I give thee my promise, thou shalt in truth

come to me, because thou art dear to me.'[63] This opens up a
new horizon, it reveals a movement of love in the divine
being.

There is always a danger that the divine being or absolute
reality should be conceived in static terms. It is infinite,
eternal, unchanging, beyond the flux of time and the
divisions of space, beyond all imagination and all thought. It
is truth, knowledge, infinity – *satyam, jnanam, anantam*.[64] It is
being, knowledge and bliss – *saccidananda* – and this concept
of bliss may suggest a movement in the divine being, but it
has often been interpreted simply as the bliss of pure
consciousness, and again therefore can be conceived as a static
mode of existence. But when the concept of love is
introduced into the divine nature, then *ananda* can be
interpreted as the bliss of love.

But how is this to be understood? In the Hindu tradition,
the divine nature has always been conceived as 'without
duality' (*advaita*): it is *ekam eva advitya*, 'one only without a
second'. What then is the relation of the world to this one
reality? Is it a pure illusion without any ultimate reality, or is
it, as we have suggested, a reflection, an image of reality, the
eternal, infinite, unchanging One mirrored in the temporal,
finite, changing world? But if this is so, then all that is
reflected here in this world, all the movements which take
place in space and time, must exist in some way in that eternal
One. This would apply also to human relationships. The love
which exists between man and woman, parents and children,
friend and friend, is an image, a reflection of the love which is
in God, and has therefore an eternal aspect. Sex itself is a
reflection of divine love and has therefore always been
considered 'holy'. It is a means by which the human being
realizes something of the mystery of divine love. We have
therefore to consider that there is a dynamism of love in God.

95

All the energy in nature, of light and heat and sound and magnetism and electricity is a reflection of the energy – the *Sakti* – which exists eternally in God. All the power of life in nature, of the living cell and organism, of plant and animal, is a reflection of the life which is in God. And so also all the love in human nature, all powers of affection and devotion, all the joy of intimacy and self-surrender are manifestations of a love which is hidden in the depths of the godhead.

Let us think of it again in terms of consciousness. We can experience love in our bodies in the intimacy of sexual union. We can experience love in our souls, in an emotional experience of melting one into another, in an imaginative experience of ecstatic love, in an experience of habitual affection which transforms one's character. All these are partial experiences of divine love. But beyond these is the capacity to experience love in depth, to go beyond sense and feeling and affection, and to discover the power of an infinite love, transcending our human capacity and awakening us to the presence of the divine being in us. This is mystical love, the point at which the human and the divine meet.

In the light of this experience of love which is that of the mystics of all ages, we can begin to see how there can be love in the divine nature itself, or rather how the divine nature can itself be love. The divine nature is reality itself, total reality, in which all being is contained and from which all being at every level of existence comes. This being, this reality, is pure consciousness, being totally transparent to itself, reflecting itself not only in the world of space and time and human consciousness, but also in its own very being, a pure reflection of being on itself, possessing itself, in perfect consciousness, knowing itself in a perfect unity of being and knowing 'without duality'. But this divine being, this absolute reality, is also love; it is a communion, a self-giving in love. By knowledge we reflect ourselves and reflect the whole creation in the mirror of ourselves. But in love, we give ourselves, communicate ourselves to another, transcend ourselves in self-surrender. So also in the divine being, in the absolute reality, there is a movement of love, a self-giving, a self-surrender. God gives himself to man, communicates his own spirit, his inner self to man, but this in turn reflects a movement of self-giving, of self-surrender in the godhead; the movement of self-knowing, of self-reflection, of self-consciousness in God, is accompanied by another movement of self-giving, of self-surrender, of ecstatic love.

Let us return again to the concept of the three worlds. The physical world, it is now recognized, is a field of energies, a 'web' of interdependent relationships, in which every object is related to every other object, and the whole is present in every part. In the same way in the psychological world every person is a centre, and each participates according to its capacity in the universal consciousness, which embraces all these centres. This universal consciousness has been compared to a point which is the centre of a circle from which radii go out in all directions. All the radii are contained in this point and are related to it and each exists only in relation to it. Another illustration is that of the sun, which sends out its rays in all directions. Every created thing is a ray of this light which is diversified into all the colours of the rainbow according to the nature of the object into which it is received but remains in itself ever the same pure white light. These are only images, but they help us to see how the world both physical and psychological comes from the supreme being and reflects it according to the diversity of natures in it, while the supreme being remains ever the same, containing within itself all the multiplicity of creatures in their principles or 'ideas' in the simple unity of its being. It is in this sense that the supreme being can be said to be 'without duality'. There is nothing in all creation which is not contained within it, no form, no energy, no life, no consciousness, not dispersed in space and time but gathered into the timeless moment and the spaceless point of its own infinite and eternal being.

But the question arises, does the individual soul or consciousness survive in this ultimate state of being? Of this it must be said that every individual soul is a centre of consciousness which is open to every other and to the universal consciousness itself. In its final fulfilment it participates in the consciousness of the supreme being and reflects the other centres of consciousness in itself, but it does not cease to be a unique centre of consciousness. The very purpose of creation was that the One should be able to communicate himself to the many, that finite and temporal beings should come to participate in the infinite and eternal being and consciousness of the One and experience the bliss – *Saccidananda* – of the Supreme. And this bliss is a bliss of love. Love seeks to communicate itself, and the purpose of love would not be satisfied if there were no one to share that love.

But does this mean that there is duality in the godhead? It is here that the concept of relationship and 'co-inherence' which was developed in the Christian doctrine of the Trinity comes into play. Though there is no duality in the godhead, there is relationship – relationship of knowledge and love. By knowledge we receive the form of another being into ourselves, we become that other being, by a mutual 'co-inherence'. This is seen above all in personal relationship. By love we communicate ourselves to other persons and they communicate themselves to us. There is a mutual self-giving which is enjoyed in sexual union, but this takes place at a deeper level of consciousness, where there is a complete in-dwelling, I in you and you in me. In human life this communion is never fully realized but in the divine life this is realized in its fullness. This is what is revealed in St John's Gospel when Jesus says, 'I am in the Father and the Father in me'.[65] This is not a simple identity – he does not say, 'I am the Father' – but a relationship of knowledge and love. But at the same time, there is perfect co-inherence. The Father is in the Son and the Son in the Father in such a way that they have but one nature which is totally in each without any duality. There is no difference between the Father and the Son except that of relationship. Their nature or essence is one 'without duality', without any difference whatsoever.

It would seem that this doctrine helps us to see how there can be knowledge and love in the godhead, that is, in ultimate reality, while it remains for ever 'without duality'. But it also shows how created beings can come to share in this non-dual mode of being and consciousness.

Jesus goes on to pray for his disciples: 'that they may be one, as thou in me and I in thee, that they may be one in us.'[66] By the gift of the Spirit which manifests the non-dual nature of the godhead, the human consciousness is raised to participation in the divine consciousness. The Spirit is the feminine or receptive aspect of the godhead as the Son is the masculine or expressive aspect. The Father knows himself in the Son and communicates himself in the Spirit. The Spirit is the receptive power in the godhead, which receives the impress of the Son, the Word and the love which flows from the Father to the Son and the Son to the Father and returns it to them. But this love is not different from the non-dual being of the godhead. It is an aspect of that being which is identical in essence with it. It is this spirit which is communicated to our human spirit, so that we participate in that love, which is the very being of the godhead. As St Paul says, 'the Spirit of God bears witness with our spirit that we are children of God.'[67] By the Spirit, therefore, we are given that receptive power which enables us to participate in the inner nature of the godhead. We participate in the Son's own knowledge of the Father, and the love which flows from the Father to the Son and over the whole creation.

This concept of 'co-inherence', of the mutual indwelling of the Father in the Son and the Son in the Father through the Spirit of love, helps us to understand not only the nature of the godhead, but also the nature of human relationships within the godhead. When human nature is taken up by the Spirit into the knowledge and love of the Father and the Son, the human consciousness is opened up to the divine mode of consciousness. Each human consciousness is expanded so as to embrace all other spheres of consciousness, both of gods or angels and of men. There is a mutual interpenetration at every level. Every being becomes transparent to every other being; each one mirrors the other and the whole. This was beautifully expressed by Plotinus, when he said, 'all is transparent, nothing dark, nothing resistant, every being is lucid to every other in breadth and depth; light runs through light and each of them contains all within itself, and at the same time sees all in every other, so that everywhere there is all, and all is all and each all, and infinite the glory'.[68] This is the vision of ultimate reality which is given us in the perennial philosophy. It is common to Greece and to India, China and Arabia, and is found in the Christian doctrine of the Mystical Body of Christ, where each creature participates through the indwelling presence of the Spirit in the inner life of the godhead and each reflects the glory in the other, 'being changed from glory into glory as by the Spirit of the Lord.'[69]

III

The Judaic Revelation

I

THE MYTHOLOGY OF THE OLD TESTAMENT

When we speak about God or the absolute or the ultimate Reality, we must always remember that we are using terms of analogy. This is the law of all religious discourse. No words can ever express what God is, what is the nature of the ultimate truth. We can only use images and concepts drawn from our human experience, which always fall short of the ultimate truth. Our images and concepts are drawn from the material world and however much they are refined by reason, they still remain inadequate to describe what lies beyond the material world. Even the human soul cannot properly be described. It is known through its experience in the body and we never normally come to know ourselves as we really are.

Yet there is a mode of experience which transcends both body and soul, an experience of the Spirit, which is not merely rational and so dependent on the senses, but intuitive – a direct insight which comes not from the soul and its faculties but from the Spirit himself, the absolute, which is present in the ground of the soul of everyman and reveals itself to those who seek him. Yet when we begin to speak of that experience, we have once more to use the language of sense and reason, and the reality of that which we have experienced can never properly be expressed.

This limitation imposes itself on all human language. The language of the Vedas, the Upanishads and the Bhagavad Gita, as we have seen, goes as far as it is possible to go towards breaking down this barrier. *Brahman, Atman* and *Purusha* are words which have been so refined in the fire of mystical experience, that they indicate with extraordinary power and precision the nature of that ultimate reality to which they bear witness, but only a leap of faith, an awakening of intuitive insight, can take us beyond the words to the truth which they signify. It is the same with the language of the Bible. The Bible grew up in the Semitic world of the Middle East, which is very different from the world of ancient India and the Far East. It has its own images and concepts, symbols derived from the unique experience of the people of Israel, but these words and symbols are all historically conditioned. The Bible is often described as the word of God, but it is the word of God expressed through the words of men with the inevitable limitation of all human words. Only by faith, that is by an intuitive understanding, which goes beyond the letter to the spirit, which enables us to share in the experience of the prophets and sages of the Old Testament, can we learn something of that truth, of that reality, to which they sought to bear witness.

When I first began to read the Bible, it was as literature, as a work of imagination, that it appealed to me, and now when I come back to it today it is as a work of supreme imagination that it still appeals to me. There is history and morality, and some philosophy and theology in the Bible, but essentially it is a work of imaginative genius in the deep sense given to the word imagination by Wordsworth and Coleridge, an insight into ultimate reality, or as Blake put it in more poetic language 'the divine body of the Lord Jesus, who is blessed forever'. In other words, the language of the imagination is part of the process of incarnation. God, the supreme reality, is manifesting himself in the whole creation.

Every material thing is a kind of incarnation, an expression in terms of matter and energy and life of the one supreme reality. In the human soul this one reality, this supreme truth, reflects itself first in the imagination, in those archetypal images which structure our consciousness. It is through these primordial images, expressed in symbols, that truth gradually reveals itself and God becomes known to man. Before being revealed as Logos or Reason, truth makes itself known through the Mythos, the Image. It is in this sense that we can speak of a mythology of the Old Testament. The Bible habitually uses the language of myth and symbol and even when there is a historical basis for a story, it is worked over by the imagination and transformed into a myth, that is, into a symbolic expression of ultimate reality.

It is a mistake to imagine that the language of abstract reason takes us nearer to God or reality than that of the concrete imagination. Goethe has well written that 'a man born and bred in the so-called exact sciences, on the height of his analytical reason, will not easily comprehend that there is such a thing as an exact concrete imagination'.[1] The Western world has been dominated for centuries now by the 'analytical reason' manifested in the 'so-called exact sciences', so that it is almost incapable of understanding the language of the imagination.

Yet all the great scriptures of the world, the Bible, the Vedas, the Koran, were written in poetic, that is symbolic, language and it is by that alone that any real knowledge, as distinguished from what Newman called 'notional' knowledge, of ultimate truth can be obtained. The language of myth and poetry, of the concrete imagination, engages the senses, the feelings, the affections and the will as well as the reason, and so leads to the transformation of the whole man. It is in this sense that the language of the imagination can be said to be a kind of incarnation.

St Thomas Aquinas translated the biblical revelation into the formal concepts of the analytical reason. It was a superb achievement and has permanent value, but these abstract concepts can never take the place of the rich imaginative language of the Bible, just as the 'dogmas' or abstract formulas of faith are a poor substitute for the living symbols of the New Testament.

It is, then, as a work of imaginative genius that we have to approach the biblical revelation, or in other words as a mythology. The word 'myth' today has lost its pejorative sense, and it is universally recognized that myth is the language of imaginative insight into ultimate reality, which not only reveals the truth under a symbol, but also enables those who receive the myth to participate in the experience of the poet or prophet who communicates it.

To know a myth in the proper sense is to be initiated into a unique experience of reality. We know how the life of primitive tribal people is dominated by the myth, which has come down from past ages and is transmitted by seers who have themselves experienced the mystery enshrined in the myth. It is in the same way that the myth of the Old Testament was revealed to the patriarchs and prophets and transmitted through the scriptures, so that every Israelite could participate in the divine mystery, which had been revealed to his ancestors. This is an organic process. The myth gradually grows in the process of transmission, as new insights are received by prophet or seer, and its ultimate meaning is gradually realized. This process did not stop with the Old Testament, but on the contrary, according to Christian belief, it was in Jesus of Nazareth that the myth of the Old Testament was given its final and definitive meaning.

A myth has always a threefold meaning. It has first of all a basis either in nature or in history, that is, in the phenomenal world. It has secondly a psychological meaning, an application to human experience both individual and social. Thirdly, it has a spiritual meaning, reflecting some aspect of ultimate truth or reality. There are nature myths in the Old Testament, above all that of creation in the first chapter of Genesis, leading on to the myth of the new creation, culminating in the new heaven and the new earth of the Revelation of St John.

But in Israel the myth always tends to have a basis in history and, unlike the Indian tradition, the historical basis grows continually in importance. Even the story of Adam and Eve, which, of course, has no basis in history, and is a pure myth, a symbolic story, revealing the original state of man and his fall into his present condition, is given a pseudo-historical basis and linked up with succeeding generations as they came down in Hebrew folklore. The story of the Flood and the tower of Babel, though essentially mythological, may have some basis in history. But when we come to the patriarchs, the founding fathers of Israel, we enter more definitely into the world of history.

Though the stories of the patriarchs seem to have been pieced together from different legendary sources,[2] they almost certainly do have a basis in history, like the stories of the *Ramayana* and the *Mahabharata* in India and the *Iliad* and *Odyssey* of Homer in Greece. But what is remarkable here is the imaginative development of these stories. Here we can see

The Marriage of East and West

the creative imagination of the Hebrew people at work, giving a profound psychological character to the stories and above all seeing them as revelations of the divine guidance in the history of Israel. In the story of Moses and the Exodus we are still in the world of myth but the historical basis is firmer and the imaginative genius of the Hebrew people, inspired by the great prophets, has left a record of the revelation of Yahweh as the God of Israel and of the awakening of the Hebrews to their identity as a people, having their own law given them by God.

Yahweh, of course, like the older Elohim, is originally a mythological figure. His association with the clouds and thunder on Mount Sinai suggests that he was at first a thunder-god like Indra in India, and Zeus and Jupiter in Greece and Rome. Later he became the tribal god of Israel taking his place among the other gods. But Yahweh soon came to be identified with the Elohim. Elohim is a word which can be compared to the Hindu Brahman. It signifies the sacred mystery, the sphere of the 'holy' as Rudolf Otto called it, the world of the gods. It is significant that the word 'Elohim' is plural and clearly goes back to a time when Israel recognized many gods. It can even be used of a ghost, as when the witch of Endor calls up the ghost of Samuel.[3] In other words it signified the supernatural world, the world of spirits. Only gradually did Israel come to recognize that Yahweh was the one God and the name Elohim, now used as a singular, could be given to him alone. In this respect the development of religion in Israel was the opposite of that in India. In India it came to be recognized that all the gods (*devas*) were names and forms of the one God, the supreme reality, who has no name and no form. In Israel the name of Yahweh was given to the one God and all the other gods were considered first of all as inferior to him[4] and then as

106

nothing compared with him.[5] But a world of spirits was also recognized, of angels and demons, corresponding to the *devas* and *asuras* of Indian tradition, and probably derived from Persian influence during the Babylonian captivity.

What distinguishes the Judaic revelation from the Vedic revelation is the emphasis on the moral character of Yahweh. The Brahman in Hinduism was described as *Saccidananda* – being, consciousness and bliss, and the emphasis was always on consciousness. For the Hindu the ascent to God is an ascent to a higher level of consciousness and eventually to the supreme consciousness which is also perfect bliss. This, of course, implied a growth in morality, and *dharma* or righteousness was seen as a necessary condition of a higher consciousness. Krishna in the Bhagavad Gita, the figure of the personal God, who is also called the 'Supreme Brahman', is said to be the 'guardian of the eternal law' (*sanatana dharma*). But the absolute is normally conceived in terms of being, truth and bliss and of non-duality rather than in terms of righteousness.

The God of Israel, on the other hand, is essentially a 'holy' god, whose characteristics are righteousness (*sadiq*) and loving-kindness (*hesed*). It is true that Yahweh was originally conceived as a very imperfect moral being, depending on the moral standards of the Hebrew people. There is a daemonic aspect of Yahweh shown in the strange story of his 'seeking to kill' Moses[6] and actually killing Uzzah in his anger because he touched the ark of God.[7] Even more serious is the story of the Passover, where Yahweh is said to 'pass over' the houses of the Israelites because they have blood on their doorposts, while he ruthlessly slays the first-born of the Egyptians.[8] Finally, and most shocking of all, is the observance of the *herem*, by which a whole city was to be destroyed and its men, women and children slaughtered as an act of devotion to

Yahweh.[9] In the course of time the anger of Yahweh was seen more and more as a judgement on sin, yet even in the great prophets the judgement of God is seen falling without discrimination on whole nations and peoples and this concept is carried over even into the New Testament, especially in the Book of Revelation.

Thus Judaism and Christianity, together with Islam, which inherited the same tradition, have always had to contend with the concept of a wrathful deity, whose actions often cannot be squared with elementary morality and whose judgements seem very remote from the requirements of love. The same problem of the 'terrible' aspect of God is found in Hinduism, with its concept of Siva the destroyer and Kali the goddess of wrath with face dripping with blood, surrounded by snakes and hung with human heads and skulls. Yet Siva is also the 'destroyer of sin' and the god of infinite grace, and Kali is the Mother, the embodiment of love and bliss. Thus each religion contends with this problem of justice and mercy, wrath and love, law and grace, and in a sense the conflict can never be resolved, as long as we remain on the level of duality.

It is only when we pass beyond the dualities that we can find the final reconciliation. Perhaps the problem is most acute with the Christian doctrine of hell and eternal punishment. In both Hinduism and Buddhism hell is a temporary state and none is condemned to eternal punishment. But the Christian doctrine of hell is firmly embedded in the New Testament and in the teaching of Jesus himself, above all in the otherwise beautiful parable of the last judgement.[10] The reason for this would seem to be that the Hebrew mind could not conceive of eternity as a state beyond time. Eternity was always imagined as an extension in time, 'for ever and ever'. This is the defect of the Hebrew mind. The imagination was marvellously developed and could penetrate into the deepest levels of reality, but the metaphysical mind which is so strong in the Hindu and the Greek, the capacity to go beyond both images and concepts and experience the timeless spaceless being beyond, was lacking in the Hebrew and it would seem in the Semitic mind. As a result both heaven and hell are conceived in spatial and temporal terms. Jesus was, of course, deliberately speaking in parables and his language is always symbolic, but in the course of time it was taken with terrible literalness. The result was the doctrine of everlasting punishment, which is surely the most terrible doctrine ever preached by any religion.

It is here that one can see the importance of understanding the Judaic revelation in terms of mythology. A myth is a symbolic story springing from the depths of human experience of the world of nature and of history in which man is involved. As such it has a power of organic growth depending on the development of the rational and moral consciousness in man under the guidance or inspiration of the Spirit within. As human consciousness develops the myth is recast and reinterpreted, often assimilating new elements and discarding old, as the Spirit leads. We can watch this process in the evolution of the Old Testament, as the epic story of Israel, its exodus from Egypt, its journey through the desert, its entry into the promised land, was rewritten and reinterpreted by successive generations. From the time of Solomon (900 BC) to the time of the return from exile in Babylon (500 BC), the story was written up no less than four times, as new insights into the meaning of Israel's history and its place in the plan of God were given through the inspired prophets.[11] By the time of David and Solomon, Israel has emerged into the light of history and the myth has now a clear historical foundation, but it does not therefore lose its mythical character.

A new myth of the Messiah and his kingdom arose out of the historical conditions of Israel in the time of David, when David was anointed as king, as Messiah, the 'anointed one', and the kingdom of Israel was firmly established.[12] But when the kingdom was divided after the death of Solomon, and Israel was again subjected to foreign rule, the myth of the Messiah and his kingdom was projected, not into the past, as with the myth of the Exodus, but into the future. A new king would come like David and re-establish the kingdom of Israel.[13] It is this myth which continues into the New Testament with the promise made to Mary that her son would be given the throne of his father David and reign over the house of Jacob.[14]

Once we have grasped the mythological character of the Bible story, everything falls into place. From beginning to end, from the story of the creation of the world and the fall of man in Genesis, through the stories of Noah and the Flood, of the patriarchs, Abraham, Isaac and Jacob, the Exodus under Moses and the journey through the desert, of the entry into the promised land and the establishment of the kingdom under David, and finally the building of the temple under Solomon, when Israel reaches the height of its greatness, the history of Israel is seen as an epic story, in which the purpose of God in the creation of man is revealed. The story has a historic basis which grows firmer as time goes on, but always it is the symbolic meaning, the revelation of the action of the Spirit of God in human history, which is of primary importance.

This is what underlies the 'allegorical' meaning of the Bible as understood by the Fathers of the Church. The literal or historical sense was always considered fundamental –

though often a historic value was given to stories like those of the book of Genesis, which was foreign to their real character – but the moral or psychological sense, the application of the story to the moral and spiritual life of man, was considered even more important. Above all was the allegorical and analogical sense, the significance of the story for the final purpose of human history and the ultimate end of man. We owe to Origen, the great biblical exegete of the third century, a magnificent conception of this universal meaning of the scriptures, but in recent times with the growth of rationalism in Europe, a crude attachment to the literal historical sense has prevailed. Only now, with a deeper understanding of the meaning and value of myth and the organic growth of the religious consciousness are we able to recover something of this profound understanding of the Bible, as of other scriptures and traditions. We are now in a position to consider the great themes of the Old Testament as the elements of a great myth, a symbolic story based on history in varying degrees but always seeking to reveal the ultimate purpose of human history, and the ultimate meaning of man and the universe.

II

THE MYTH OF THE NEW CREATION

The Bible begins with the story of the creation of the world in the book of Genesis when 'God created the heavens and the earth' and ends with the story of the new creation in the book of the Revelation of St John when he says: 'I saw a new heaven and a new earth'.[15] The whole story of the Bible is thus set within the context of the cosmic myth of creation, destruction and re-creation. But this is not as in the ancient myth of the 'eternal return', a cyclic movement of emanation and dissolution, to be followed by another period of emanation and dissolution, but a movement of progress to a final state. The new creation of the Revelation is not a state which is to be followed by another stage of dissolution, but the final consummation of all things, in which the whole creation is taken up into the divine life, passing beyond its present state of existence in space and time into its final state of fulfilment, when as St Paul says, 'all things will be brought to a head, things in heaven and things on earth.'[16] This is the plan of God revealed progressively in the Old Testament and realized fully in the New. It is not only all humanity which is envisaged in this plan, but the whole creation, both heaven and earth. Further, by heaven the Bible does not mean simply the sky. As we have seen, in the ancient world matter was never conceived apart from mind, conscious and unconscious were held together in organic unity by the power of the supreme Spirit. Heaven, therefore, was not simply the sky, but the abode of God. When Jesus taught his disciples to pray 'Our father in heaven', he was speaking not of the material but of the spiritual heaven, or rather he was using the word in its primordial sense as the abode of God, the supreme Spirit, which embraces the material and the spiritual world in an organic unity.

The seven days of creation were variously interpreted in the early Church. The school of Antioch, of which St John Chrysostom was representative, held to the literal interpretation, supposing the whole world to have been created literally in seven days, but the school of Alexandria, with Clement and Origen at its head, found the meaning of the scriptures mainly in the 'allegorical' or symbolic sense. For them the whole creation was considered to have come forth from God in a single act of the divine power, and the seven days was merely an accommodation of the mystery of creation to human understanding. But there was another school, represented by St Gregory of Nyssa in the East and St Augustine in the West, which held with the school of Alexandria that the world was created at a moment of time by a single act of the divine power, but that it was produced not in the form in which we know it but in its 'potentiality'. According to St Gregory of Nyssa, God created not the forms of things as they now exist but certain 'powers' or 'energies' which were destined to develop in the course of time into the present forms of nature. The seven days of creation were interpreted simply as the stages in the evolution of these primordial energies according to what he called a 'necessary order'. In the same way St Augustine spoke of the world being created in its 'causes' or 'seminal principles' (*rationes seminales*), that is to say that certain principles were implanted in nature from the beginning like seeds, which were destined to develop their specific forms according to the laws or tendencies inherent in them. It can be seen how close this comes to a modern evolutionary view of the universe.[17]

According to this view, the whole creation is seen to evolve from certain elementary principles, powers or causes, which were created by God in the beginning and were destined to develop into the forms of nature, as we know them, according to their own intrinsic law. The whole process was set in motion by the divine power and directed throughout the course of its evolution by the divine wisdom, so as to form an organic whole following its own intrinsic laws. In this process man was seen to be the final term of evolution. For the body of man is linked with the whole course of evolution and marks the limit of the unfolding of those original powers of nature. But at the same time this body is informed by a rational soul, which raises him above the order of nature, and gives him a direct relation with God. Thus man stands between the material and spiritual worlds, partaking of the nature of each and forming the link between them. This is essentially the position of man according to the Christian view. He stands at the head of nature, bringing all the original powers of nature to their highest point of development, so that in him those energies which had been working unconsciously in the heart of matter from the beginning, now become conscious. Nature in him receives a new direction and opens out on the world of the spirit. Nature, we may say, becomes conscious in man. But what is the end of this process, what is the term of this development? This is a question neither science nor philosophy can answer. Philosophers may play with the idea of a 'superman', but it is clearly beyond their power to conceive what his nature would be. For a new stage in evolution must transcend our present state of consciousness, no less than the present state of man transcends that of an animal, or that of an animal transcends that of a plant.

If there is a higher state of being than that of man it can only be made known to us by a revelation from a higher state of consciousness. Every religious tradition reveals something of this transcendent state, and the biblical revelation can be seen as a gradual unfolding of this mystery of a 'new creation', a passage beyond this present world into a new state of being and consciousness.

This passage from time to eternity, from creation to new creation, was symbolized in the story of creation by the 'rest' of God. 'And God rested', it is said, 'on the seventh day from all his works'.[18] The six days of creation represent the week of time and of earthly activity, while the seventh day is the day of eternity, when all labour ceases. The Sabbath was intended to be a perpetual reminder of the rest which awaits us at the end of our labours in this world. It was also a reminder to the people of Israel of the rest which awaited them in the promised land. But this land, which had at first been conceived in terms of the land of Canaan, the Palestine which has remained a source of contention in the world until the present day, gradually revealed its deeper significance. The land in the ancient world could never be conceived as a merely material thing. The land is a home, a dwelling place where man discovers his deep relation with the cosmic order. It is also the place where he discovers God, as Jacob did when he lay down and slept and saw a ladder reaching up to heaven and angels ascending and descending on it, and said when he awoke 'Surely the Lord is in this place and I knew it not'.[19] The 'land' thus becomes the symbol of man's hope of a final resting place, the land of heart's desire. It was so that it came to be seen as the 'heavenly country', where the city of God is to be found.[20]

But this land of promise is something more than the fulfilment of human destiny, it is the fulfilment of creation. Already in the last stages of Hebrew prophecy it had been declared: 'Behold, I create new heavens and a new earth, and the former things shall not be remembered or come into mind. But be glad and rejoice in that which I create, for behold, I create Jerusalem a rejoicing and her people a joy.'[21] Here we can begin to see the full significance of the new creation. It involves a transformation of 'heaven and earth', that is, of the whole cosmic order, as we now conceive it in our limited spatial and temporal consciousness. St Paul, in the letter to the Romans, gives us a wonderful picture of the whole creation 'groaning in travail' while it 'waits for the revealing of the sons of God'. 'For the creation itself will be set free from its bondage to decay and obtain the glorious liberty of the children of God'.[22] In this view the whole creation, that is the material world, is destined to undergo a radical transformation, as it participates in the transformation of human consciousness and of human society symbolized by Jerusalem, the City of God.

This transformation will take place when both the body and soul of man have been transformed by the in-dwelling Spirit. Man is a psychosomatic unity, a body-soul, and as the soul, that is, human consciousness, is transformed by the power of the Spirit, so the body also will be transformed. That structure of energies which makes up our present mode of being will be changed, and with it the whole field of energies of which the human body is a part. Just as man is a psychosomatic being, a body penetrated by consciousness, so the whole cosmos is a psychosomatic unity, a field of energies penetrated by consciousness. At present this consciousness in nature is latent, just as the consciousness of our bodies is latent and incomplete. But in the final state, the body of man will be totally penetrated by consciousness and become a 'spiritual body', and at the same time the material world with all its energies now penetrated by consciousness will become a 'new creation'.

This is the vision of the seer of the Revelation of St John, when he writes: 'I saw a new heaven and a new earth, for the first heaven and the first earth had passed away . . . and he who sat on the throne said "Behold, I make all things new".'[23] He who 'sat on the throne' is, of course, the Lord or the Spirit who dwells in man, enthroned above our present consciousness. This Spirit has been present in nature from the beginning, building up the world of matter, penetrating it first with vital energies and then with consciousness. Now, taking up its throne in the midst of the cosmos, it raises our human mind and will to participation in its own infinite and eternal mode of being, and with man raises the whole material world to conscious participation in the divine mode of being. This is the end of the whole creative process, the passage beyond the present spatial and temporary order. In this process nothing is lost. The present creation is not simply dissolved but is re-created. All the latent powers in nature and in man, which in the present world order are doomed to frustration, are there realized in their plenitude. Our present mode of consciousness is essentially transitional. It is a temporary state between animal consciousness and divine consciousness. In the final state all the limitations and frustrations of this present life will be overcome and the whole creation will enter into the state of divine bliss. In this state 'death will be no more, neither shall there be mourning nor crying nor pain any more, for the former things have passed away.'[24] This is the return to Paradise from which man had been cast out in the beginning, the recovery of the original state of man and the universe, of which the second letter of Peter says: 'according to his promise we wait for new heavens and a new earth, in which righteousness dwells.'[25]

III

THE MYTH OF PARADISE LOST

'The Lord God planted a garden in the East in Eden.'[26] The myth of the Garden of Eden is one of the most beautiful and significant in the Bible and indeed in all human history. It has all the elements of an archetypal myth, the garden and the tree, the serpent and the man and the woman. The significance of this myth is inexhaustible, but we can suggest some of its meaning for man today. There is first of all the garden, symbol of the original harmony of man's environment. Man was originally a child of nature. He was formed 'of the dust of the ground', the same ground from which 'the Lord God (that is, Yahweh, Elohim) made to grow every tree that is pleasant to the sight and good for food.'[27] Man is thus part of this world of nature and has an intrinsic bond with it. Ancient man always strove to preserve this bond. The earth was his mother and in everything this harmony with nature had to be preserved. Modern man has broken this bond and sought to exploit nature by every means in his power. The disastrous effects on the ecology of our environment are the price which we are paying for this sin, the original sin of man's revolt against nature.

Man was allowed to eat of all the fruits of the trees in the garden, but of the fruit of the Tree of Knowledge of good and evil, he could not eat. What is the meaning of this? The Tree of Knowledge of good and evil is the tree of wisdom, and it stands close to the tree of life, which is the tree of immortality. Wisdom and immortality were the two gifts offered by God to man, but they had to be received as a gift; the moment man sought to seize them for himself, he would die. This is the drama of human existence. Man has a body formed from the 'dust of the ground' and a soul which he received from God. 'The Lord God breathed into his nostrils the breath of life; and man became a living soul.'[28] The soul of man is a 'breath' or 'spirit' from God. By it man is raised above the animal world and is able to partake of the Spirit of God. But he has to receive this spirit, this life, as a gift. It is not under his control. The other faculties of the soul, the senses, the feelings, the imagination are under his control and he can eat of their fruit, but the Spirit is from God and he cannot appropriate it to himself.

This is the original sin of man which is repeated daily in human experience. It has been repeated on a vaster scale than ever before in the present day. Never before has man made a determined effort to become master of his own destiny, to take in hand, as they say, the future of evolution. He is learning to 'master' the powers of nature and is seeking to gain control of the human psyche by genetic engineering. He has a vision of himself as the master of the universe. This is the sin of Prometheus, who stole fire from heaven. It is the *hubris*, the pride, which the Greeks knew to be the source of disaster. The threat of a nuclear war which may destroy the earth is the inevitable result of this sin. The root of it lies in the attempt to separate the human soul from its bond with nature and with the Spirit. The human soul with its powers of reason and free will is a reflection of the Spirit of God in man. The Spirit is the source, the ground of all being. Every thing comes from the Spirit and reflects its power and light. The energy of matter, the life in plants and animals, the soul in man are all reflections, effects of the power and life and knowledge, of the one Spirit. To recognize the dependence of all creation on the inner light and power of the Spirit is to partake of the Spirit's own wisdom and immortality. But to refuse to recognize this dependence, to seek to be autonomous and to control the world, is to take the path of death. The story of Genesis is but one example of a myth that was known to all ancient peoples. The image of the two birds on the tree of the Svetasvatara Upanishad tells the same story. The one bird, the human soul, eats of the fruit of the tree and grows sad and bewildered, but when it looks up and sees the other, the Lord, the Spirit within, its grief passes away.

But there are two other actors in this drama: the serpent and the woman. What are they? The serpent represents the animal intelligence, the wisdom of the earth. This is the wisdom of modern science. It is a wisdom which comes not from above but below. It comes from man's immersion in the material world, seeking to extract its secrets so as to increase his own power. It corresponds closely with magic in the ancient world and there is, in fact, evidence that Western science evolved at the Renaissance, along with magic.[29] Its essential character in any case is the same, to gain control over the powers of nature and exploit them for man's benefit but also for man's destruction. Both in magic and in science, however, there is an ambivalence. To gain control over the powers of nature in order to bring both man and nature under the guidance and control of the Spirit within, can make both science and magic instruments of human progress, but the temptation is always there to become like God: 'You shall be as God knowing good and evil.'[30] But this again is ambivalent. There is a sense in which the very purpose of creation was that man should become like God, sharing in his wisdom and immortality, but this can only come when man surrenders all the powers of his being, of body and soul, to the power of the Spirit within. Then he works in harmony with nature; body and soul, conscious and unconscious, are united and integrated, and man and nature co-operate with the indwelling Spirit, who rules everything from within. This is the original Paradise, the state to which man was first called and to which he continues to aspire today.

Finally, we come to the woman. 'The woman gave me fruit of the tree and I did eat,' says the man in the story of Genesis.[31] Who and what is this woman? Woman represents the intuitive power in human nature while man represents the rational mind. These are two complementary aspects of human nature and a human being is only complete when these two functions of human nature have been 'married'. It is important to recognize that these functions are complementary; both are equally necessary. Man and woman are equal and opposite. A woman does not become more equal to man by seeking to become like a man, but by revealing his opposite character. Yet it must be recognized that every man and woman is both male and female; reason and intuition exist alike in every human being, but in the man reason is dominant and intuition is subordinate, while in woman intuition is dominant and reason is subordinate. In a perfect man or woman the 'marriage' of the opposites takes place, and in fact the very purpose of an exterior marriage is to enable the man and the woman to complete one another by an interior marriage. On the other hand, when reason and intuition, the man and woman, are separated, then disaster follows. Reason without intuition is intelligent but sterile, intuition without reason is fertile but blind. The woman who seduces man is the blind intuition which listens to the voice of the serpent, the animal intelligence, or sexuality. This is the normal course of sin. The feminine mind, instead of being guided by reason so as to open itself to the Spirit and so to achieve the marriage of intuition and reason and the integration of the personality, surrenders to animal instinct and drags the reason down with it. The serpent certainly has a sexual significance, but it is not that sex is evil. Sex is an animal instinct which, when the woman surrenders to the man and the man to the woman, becomes the means of their communion in the Spirit. Thus the serpent becomes the Saviour, as it was said in St John's Gospel, 'As Moses lifted up the serpent in the wilderness, so must the Son of Man be lifted up, that whoever believes in him may have eternal life.'[32] It is the separation of sex from intuition or feeling and from reason and understanding, which is the cause of sin, while the integration of the sexual instinct with feeling and imagination – that is the intuitive mind – and with reason and will – that is the rational mind – brings about fulfilment both of man and woman in the life of the Spirit. It is in this way that man truly becomes like God, or rather actually participates in the life of God.

We can now begin to see the original structure of human nature, its state of original justice, as it has been called. First of all, man, that is the human being, is created in harmony with nature, as an element in the vast system of energies which stretches from this earth to the farthest stars. But at the same time man has in him the breath of the Spirit of God, a capacity of reason and free will, a specifically human consciousness, which raises him above the whole material world, and gives him the capacity to know himself and the world in which he lives. It is this capacity which makes man an image of God with the ability to become 'like God'. But this man is both man and woman, as it is said: 'God created man in his own image, in the image of God he created him; male and female he created them.'[33] Every man is both man and woman, the sexual differentiation enabling him to be human in a characteristically different way. The modern movement towards women's liberation is right in so far as it seeks to enable woman to become fully human in a specifically feminine way, but it would be disastrous if it were to lead to a loss of the differentiation of the sexes. A woman is human in a specifically feminine way and a man in a specifically masculine way. But finally both nature and man are created to become 'like God' by the indwelling presence of the Spirit. Man, as we have seen, is both soul and spirit. Both body and soul, both man and nature, depend for their very existence on the power of the Spirit, which transcends both man and nature, both matter and human consciousness. It is this eternal Spirit, source of matter and life and consciousness, which in the Bible is given the name of God.

Both man and nature are evolving in time and space, and

the purpose of the whole evolutionary process is that both man and nature should come to participate in the infinite and eternal being of the one Supreme Spirit or God. Sin has entered into this evolutionary process and introduced a principle of disorder, a separation between man and nature, between man and woman, between man and God. The myth of the Garden of Eden is a symbolic story revealing both the original state of man, that is, the original structure of human nature, and the 'fall' of man, the failure of man to respond to the call of his nature, to become one with God and live by the life of the Spirit. The Bible goes on to tell of the consequences of this fall, the alienation of man from nature – 'cursed is the ground for your sake; in sorrow shall you eat all the days of your life'[34] – the domination of women by man and the pain of child-bearing – 'in sorrow you shall bring forth children'.[35] But it is then that the great myth of redemption begins, the story of man's deliverance from sin and restoration to Paradise, the myth of *Paradise Regained*.

IV

THE MYTH OF THE PROMISED LAND

The story begins with the promise of the land. 'Go from your country,' it is said, 'and from your kindred and your father's house, to the land that I will show you.'[36] Man had been cast out of the Garden of Eden and an angel with a flaming sword was set to bar the way to the tree of life.[37] There was no way of return to lost innocence, the way lay forward through the trials and conflicts of this world to another land. We must never forget that the Bible represents the story of mankind in its relation with God. It begins with the first man, Adam, and ends with the second Adam, the New Man. Adam is the representative of mankind. St Paul calls him the *tupos tou mellontos*, the figure or type of him who was to come,[38] and human history is the story of the passage of man from his primordial state of innocence to his final state of perfection, of 'mature manhood'.[39]

This passage is represented as a journey to a promised land, and it is significant that Israel was a pastoral people, a nomadic tribe, always going from place to place in search of pasture. This is indicated at the beginning in the story of Cain and Abel, when the first effect of sin is seen as a conflict between the pastoral and the agricultural peoples. For Abel, it is said, 'was a keeper of sheep', but Cain was a 'tiller of the ground'.[40]

The agricultural peoples represent the great settled civilizations of antiquity, in particular Babylon and Egypt, who settled in the river valleys and built up great civilizations. To them we owe not only agriculture, but also pottery and weaving, metal work and engineering, commerce and banking, as well as mathematics and astronomy. Depending on the earth and their own industry for their prosperity, they turned to the worship of the Earth, the great Mother, and all the powers of nature. They are the forerunners of the 'great powers' of the modern world. But Israel was a pastoral people, living in tents and journeying from place to place.[41] Depending on the rain from heaven for their livelihood, they worshipped the God of heaven and learned their radical dependence on him.

In this way the Hebrews were led to see their status as a pastoral people 'dwelling in tents' as symbolic of their position as the 'people of God', having no 'abiding city' in this world but living as 'pilgrims and strangers' on earth because they are seeking the city of God.[42] Thus the great division of mankind was begun, as St Augustine saw it in his

City of God, between those who make their home in this world and seek salvation through the powers of nature, that is through science and technology, and those who are in search of another country, another world, to which the Spirit is leading us, where above all human fulfilment is to be found. This is the significance of the promise made to Abraham. He is to leave his country and his father's house and go in search of a land, and there he will become a great people and in him 'all the races of the world will be blessed'.[43]

It is important to observe that from the beginning the promise was made on behalf of 'all the races of the world'. Though Israel was chosen to be the 'people of God', there was never any question but that this was so that it should be the source of salvation for all mankind. St Paul in his letter to the Romans makes a great point of this, that the promise was made to Abraham before he was circumcised, that is, before he was marked off as a Jew, so that he might be the 'father of all who believe'. In this sense Abraham is the father not only of the Jew and the Christian and the Muslim, who all acknowledge him as the father of their faith, but of all those who seek God or some transcendent state or value, which only faith can recognize. Thus the universality of the divine promise was made clear from the beginning. Abraham is the representative of mankind, which receives in him the promise of salvation, and begins to be formed into a people through whom the human race will be reconciled with God. This people will be educated by the Law and taught by the prophets, that it may be prepared for the reception of the Spirit of God. But in all this it is mankind which is being taught and trained and prepared for its destiny, so that the history of Israel is the story of mankind.

Israel, then, is a people which has been called out of the

world to go in search of a land. The promise to Abraham was renewed to Isaac[44] and again to Jacob.[45] Then begins the drama of the descent into Egypt with Joseph, and Israel is once again enslaved to the powers of this world. But then the promise is renewed to Moses: 'I will bring you out from under the burdens of the Egyptians, and I will deliver you from their bondage . . . and I will take you for my people . . . and I will bring you into the land which I swore to give to Abraham, to Isaac and to Jacob; I will give it to you for a possession.'[46] So Israel sets out again on its journey to the promised land and after all the trials of the journey through the desert the promise is renewed to Joshua: 'Be strong and of good courage, for you shall cause this people to inherit the land, which I swore to their fathers to give them.'[47] This is the drama of human liberation, the enslavement to the powers of this world, the economic and social systems, whether capitalist or communist, which enslave mankind by subjecting it to the forces of the material world; the long journey through the desert, which separation from these powers involves, and finally the entry into the promised land.

But now the story takes a new turn. Israel conquers the land and settles in it, builds houses and plants vineyards. It is given a king and a law to govern it, and a temple is built in which their God can dwell. It seems that all the promises have been fulfilled. They have taken possession of the land, have conquered their enemies and become a great people, and have built a temple where God can dwell among them for ever. But now begins what Aristotle called the *peripateia* in a tragedy, the reversal of fortune which brings disaster. The Assyrians come up and conquer northern Israel (what today is the West Bank), and the people are carried away captive. Then the Babylonians come and capture Jerusalem. The temple is destroyed, the king and people are taken captive and go into exile. The land is left desolate. All the promises seem to have failed, and Israel is left in a worse form of slavery than ever. We touch at this point the heart of the mystery of human existence. Why is it that all human enterprise and all human civilization is doomed to failure? Why this continual breakdown with which we are faced at every level of life, individual and social, political and religious? This is the question which faces us today, as it has faced every civilization.

The answer is given in the history of Israel. The settlement in the land under Joshua and the establishment of the Kingdom under David and Solomon – and the same must be said of the settlement of Israel in its land today – could never be anything but a temporary phenomenon. Human destiny does not lie in the temporal and material order, and every temporal achievement can only be a preparation in time for what is to be achieved in eternity.

So it was that at this time of desolation, when God seemed to have deserted his people, the great prophets arose to proclaim that Israel would once again return to the land; there would be another king like David, and another temple like that of Solomon. Again the prophecy was at first seen in temporal terms – there was a return to the land, and though the kingdom was not restored, yet a new temple was built and the old religion continued as before. But the prophets were looking beyond this. They saw that there must be a new law and a new covenant, a law which would be 'written on the heart'.[48] There was to be a life beyond the grave, when the people would be given a 'new heart and a new spirit'.[49] That profound transformation was taking place in Israel which at the same time took place in India with the Upanishads. An external religion based on rites and

ceremonies, requiring priesthood and sacrifice, was passing
into a religion of the spirit, in which the dwelling place of
God was seen to be not in temples made with hands but in the
human heart. 'I will put my spirit within you,' it is said, 'and
you shall live.' But again the promise of the land is renewed,
'I will place you in your own land'.[50] But what is this land
which man is to inherit? This becomes clear in the later
prophecy of Isaiah, when it was said: 'Behold, I create new
heavens and a new earth . . . and behold, I create Jerusalem a
rejoicing, and her people a joy.'[51]

The destiny of man does not lie in this world. It is beyond
time and space in an experience of being, transcending our
present human conditions. This was revealed in India in the
time of the Buddha and the Upanishads and it became clear in
Israel in the time of the great prophets. This was the moment
of breakthrough for humanity, which had been preparing in
all the ages which had gone before. It was implicit from the
beginning, because the Spirit is immanent in all creation and
is present as an active power in all religion. But the Spirit was
concealed under the forms of nature and the figures of
mythology. But now it breaks through and begins to shine
with its own light. Yet the problem remains. Though the
Spirit receives a name and is conceived as beyond all outward
forms, yet we still have to use words and images in order to
speak of it. People still need rituals and sacrifices and temples
and images to make the divine mystery real to themselves.
Yet a change has taken place. It is now known that all these
words and images are but outward signs of a hidden mystery,
and the myth and the symbol are recognized for what they
are. It is thus that today we have to look on all the myths and
symbols of religion as signs of a mystery which is beyond
word and thought and yet which reveals itself and makes
itself present through these symbols.

What, then, is the symbolism of the promised land? It is surely a symbol of the search for a 'return to nature', to that original state of harmony between man and nature. All of us once upon a time, when we were in the womb, were in perfect harmony with nature, we were part of the great Mother herself. Every human being bears in himself the memory of this original oneness, this total harmony. The child too, after it is born, if it is loved and cherished, may experience something of this original wholeness. Many primitive people also, like the pygmies in central Africa, who live very close to nature, feel themselves to be one with nature. They have an intuitive awareness of their bonds with the plants and animals and live in the cosmic harmony of day and night, summer and winter, birth and marriage and death. But as reason develops and they eat of the tree of knowledge a division grows between man and nature. Man feels himself separate from nature, the world becomes his enemy, violence and conflict take the place of the original peace. But there is no going back to Eden; he cannot return to that state of innocence when his consciousness was not divided. He has to advance through trial and conflict to a communion with nature at a deeper level of consciousness. The danger is that as the rational mind develops and man becomes capable of controlling the forces of nature, he seeks to dominate nature and uses her for his own purposes. This has been the course of history in Western Europe and America, and has led to the present state of conflict, where human existence is threatened by the forces which have been released.

But there is another way, by which, as reason develops and a scientific knowledge gives man the capacity to control the forces of nature, he enters into a new relationship. The rational mind enters into communion with the intuitive mind, and man and nature are 'married'. The male ceases to dominate the female or to be seduced by her, and a marriage of equals takes place. Both the man and the woman are made whole by this marriage. The objective world is no longer an enemy to be subdued but a partner in marriage. There is a saying in one of the apocryphal gospels, 'When will the kingdom of God come?', and the answer is given 'When the two shall be one, when that which is without is as that which is within, and the male and the female shall be one.'[52] This is the return to Paradise, the reversal of the effects of the Fall.

In Paradise man had been in harmony with nature, with himself and with God. Sin had brought division between man and nature, between man and woman, and between man and God. In the plan of redemption this threefold harmony is to be restored. Therefore the promise is made to Abraham of a land where he shall dwell securely, signifying the reconciliation of man and nature. Then he shall become a great people in which all the races of the world will be blessed, signifying the restoration of mankind to its original wholeness. Finally, God will come to dwell in this people: 'You shall be my people, and I will be your God.'[53]

The symbolism of the land is brought out most clearly in the letter to the Hebrews. This letter, which is known not to be by St Paul, was probably written in Alexandria, where the tradition of Platonism with its deep sense of symbolism was preserved. Thus it is said that the gifts and sacrifices offered in the temple were only a copy and a shadow of the heavenly sanctuary.[54] All earthly rites and ceremonies are in Plato's sense 'copies' of eternal realities. So it was that the promised land came to be seen in a new light. When Abraham went out, it is said, to go to a place which he was to receive as an inheritance, he did not know where he was to go. He was journeying in search of an unknown country, seeking a homeland. The land which he was seeking was not that from which he came out, it was a 'better country, that is, a heavenly one'.[55] Here we can see the passage from the literal to the symbolic sense, from a this-worldly religion to an other-worldly religion.

Our desire for a homeland can never be satisfied with anything in this world. The passionate desire of so many people to find a homeland is a sign of this desire for something beyond this world. Yet there is a deep sense in which this desire is genuine. We do not desire a state in which there will be no earth, no bodily nature. We desire the satisfaction of our bodily desires, a communion with nature in which the profound awareness of our oneness with nature will be realized, a communion with one another in which the deepest intimacy of sexual union will be experienced. This was marvellously expressed by the prophet Isaiah when he said: 'You shall no longer be termed Forsaken, and your land Desolate, but you shall be called My delight is in her, and your land Married; for the Lord delights in you, and your land shall be married. For as a young man marries a virgin, so shall your sons marry you, and as the bridegroom rejoices over the bride, so shall your God rejoice over you.'[56]

All this takes place only in the new creation, when soul and body are transfigured by the indwelling Spirit, when the 'land' is no longer seen as an exterior object but is experienced within as the soul's eternal ground, and the man and the woman are united not in external marriage but in the interior marriage, which takes place in God, that is, in the inner depth of the Spirit, beyond time and space.

V

THE MYTH OF THE EXODUS

Man sets out on his journey to the Promised Land, and begins to build a city, to create a civilized world, but invariably his efforts meet with disaster. This is one of the main themes of the Bible, the constant failure of every human effort, the fatality that dogs man's footsteps. It is seen first of all in the story of the Flood in the book of Genesis. No sooner had men begun to multiply and fill the earth than a flood came and destroyed them all. This flood is, no doubt, a historical memory of a flood, which took place in the valley of the Tigris and Euphrates in Mesopotamia, but it is symbolic of those natural disasters which so often overwhelm the world. In the Bible it is seen as a judgement on human sin but at the same time as a token of redemption.

Waters always have this dual character. On the one hand, they represent the 'chaos', the powers of death and destruction, which are always threatening to overwhelm the world. On the other hand, they represent the powers of life and of regeneration upon which the earth depends. Psychologically, they represent the powers of the 'unconscious', the elemental passions, which lie beneath the surface of conscious life. But again these same powers when they come under the influence of the Spirit become powers of life and regeneration. The 'waters below the firmament' are drawn up 'above the firmament' and descend in life-giving showers of divine grace. So in the story of the Flood, the waters are seen not only as destroying the world but also as a symbol of baptism, that is, of death and resurrection. We have to die, to go under the waters of the unconscious, in order that we may be reborn and experience the power of a new life.

This is seen in the story of Noah. Noah is the righteous man who is saved with his wife and children by entering the Ark of Salvation. The ark represents the new creation. Noah is the new Adam, the new father of mankind, through whom humanity is saved, and with humanity the whole animal creation which enters with him into the ark. Thus it is said 'God did not spare the ancient world but preserved Noah, a herald of righteousness, with seven other persons, when he brought a flood upon the world of the ungodly.'[57] This mystery of water as the symbol at once of destruction and of regeneration is one of the principal themes of the Bible. At every stage, in the story of the Flood, the Exodus from Egypt and the entry into the Promised Land, there is a passage through the waters, a death and a judgement has to be endured, the 'old man' has to die in order that the 'new man' may be born.

This passage from death to life is the main theme of the Exodus. The children of Israel after a brief sojourn in the land of promise, go down into Egypt and there for four hundred years they remain enslaved to the powers of this world. Then comes Moses, the figure of the Saviour, who has a vision of God in the Burning Bush and is called to lead Israel out of Egypt back to the promised land. But this is only accomplished through death and destruction. Egypt is beset by plagues until finally the first-born of the Egyptians are slain, while the angel of death passes over the Israelites, who have the blood of a lamb sprinkled on the doorposts.

All of this is, of course, rich in symbolism. Egypt signifies the powers of this world, both the great cities which breed the pollution both of the earth and of human nature, and at the same time the daemonic powers at work in all great civilizations, making men blind to the life of the Spirit. The slaying of the first-born represents the conquest of these evil powers and the blood of the lamb is the symbol of the life of the Spirit, which was one day to be manifested as the blood of Jesus, shed on the Cross and restoring life to humanity. Israel's escape from Egypt and passage through the Red Sea is the liberation of man from the bondage of this world and the passage through the waters, which both drown the enemies of the soul which pursue it, and make a way for humanity to enter on a new life. This can be seen as a liberation of mankind from the oppressive powers of this world, whether capitalist or communist, and a pathway to freedom, by which man recovers his true nature and enters into communion with God.

But this pathway to freedom demands a journey through the desert. The world will not be saved by means of any manipulation of the economic or political order. There has to be a turning away from this world, an opening to the transcendent mystery of existence, if humanity is to escape from its present bondage. This is illustrated by the story of the journey through the desert. At the beginning of every great movement of the Spirit there is a departure for the desert. At the time of the Upanishads the Vedic *rishis* retired to the forest to meditate. The Buddha left home and family to become an ascetic until he found enlightenment under the Bo tree. Mahavira, the founder of the Jains, left everything to wander naked in search of liberation. John the Baptist prepared the way for the coming of Jesus by living in the desert. Jesus himself spent six weeks in the desert before he began his ministry. St Paul, after his conversion, retired for three years to the desert of Arabia. So it was that Israel, when it was to be prepared for its entry into the promised land, had to spend forty years in the wilderness. The Christian Fathers,

Origen and Gregory of Nyssa, saw the journey through the desert as a symbol of the soul's journey towards God. Origen saw it simply as the journey through the trials and temptations of this present life towards the promised land. But Gregory of Nyssa, following Philo the Jew, had a more profound understanding of it. St Paul had spoken of the Israelites being 'baptized through Moses in the cloud and in the sea'.[58] This is one of the clearest instances in the New Testament of a symbolic interpretation of the Old Testament. St Paul saw the passage through the sea as a 'type' or figure of baptism, and the presence of the cloud as a sign of the presence of the Holy Spirit.

This cloud has a long history in the Bible. It covered the tabernacle or tent, where the ark of God was kept, whenever the Israelites encamped in the desert. 'For the cloud of the Lord was upon the tabernacle by day, and there was fire therein by night in the sight of all the house of Israel throughout their journeys.'[59] Again, when the temple was built by Solomon and the ark was placed in the sanctuary containing the tables of the law 'the cloud filled the house of the Lord' and 'the glory of the Lord filled the house of the Lord'.[60]

Later, when the temple was destroyed, Ezekiel had a vision of a new temple and saw the 'glory of the Lord' descend upon it.[61] This symbolism is taken up in the New Testament, where at the transfiguration of Jesus, when the divine light shines through him, 'there came a cloud overshadowing them and a voice from the cloud'.[62]

Finally, one may mention that at the ascension of Jesus, St Luke says that 'a cloud received him out of their sight'.[63] This cloud is clearly no ordinary cloud, but a symbol of the divine presence or 'glory'. It was a sign to the people of Israel that the divine presence accompanied them throughout their journey. So it is that for every one who sets out on this journey through the desert, he first of all encounters God in the burning bush; he awakes to the mystery of the 'holy', of the divine light, which is revealing itself to him. But this light comes to him under a cloud. It is what the author of the old English mystical treatise called The Cloud of Unknowing.

Just as going out in search of God is like going into a desert, though it is really a place which contains the springs of eternal life, so the experience of the presence of God throughout the journey is like being under a cloud and in the darkness, though in reality it is a blinding light. As one comes nearer to God, the darkness deepens. This is where St Gregory of Nyssa differs from Origen. He sees the culmination of the experience of the desert in the ascent of Mount Sinai, when Moses goes up into the mountain and meets God in the darkness. 'And the glory of the Lord abode on Mount Sinai and the cloud covered it six days, and on the seventh day [the day of rest, it will be remembered, of eternity, after the six days of labour in the week of time] God called to Moses out of the midst of the cloud . . . and Moses entered into the midst of the cloud . . . and Moses was in the cloud forty days and forty nights.'[64]

St Gregory of Nyssa[65] compares the crossing of the Red Sea to Baptism and to the purgative way, the passage from the world of sin, signified by Egypt, to the new life when we are 'born again of water and the spirit'.[66] The journey through the desert guided by the Cloud, signifying the presence of the Holy Spirit, is compared to the sacrament of Confirmation and to the illuminative way, the life illumined by the presence of the Spirit and nourished by the manna, the 'bread from heaven' and the 'water from the rock', which is the water 'springing up to eternal life'.[67] Finally, the ascent of Mount Sinai is compared to the Eucharist and to the unitive way, the meeting God in the darkness, beyond sense and reason, where he reveals himself in the communion of love.

Thus the story of the Exodus has at least three levels of meaning. There is first of all the literal and historical sense, the deliverance of the people of Israel from bondage in Egypt, which is itself symbolic of the deliverance of all people from political, social and economic bondage. There is secondly the moral sense of man's separation from the world of sin, and his entry on the path of righteousness, when he receives the ten commandments of the law. Finally, there is the mystical sense of the passage from this world to the next, from the world of appearances to the world of real being, from the light of this world to the 'divine darkness' where man meets God.

This is the background to the story of the death and resurrection of Jesus. The whole story is deliberately placed in the context of the Jewish festival of the Passover. Jesus gathers his disciples around him to eat the Passover with them and there prepares them for his death, by inaugurating a 'new covenant' in his blood, thus recalling the first covenant with Moses.[68] Thus the death of Jesus is linked historically with the Exodus from Egypt. But at the same time this death is to set the people free not merely from bondage in Egypt but from bondage to sin, that is, from the bondage of this world. But St John goes further than this and shows how it is the moment of Jesus 'passing from this world to the Father'.[69] It is the moment of his entrance into 'glory', that 'glory' which Moses had asked to see[70] and which is nothing less than the radiance of the divine being.[71]

Thus the deepest meaning of the Exodus is the passing from this world, the world of shadows and of unreality, to the Father, that is, to the Source, the Origin, the One beyond the many. In the words of the Upanishads, it is the passing from the 'unreal to the real, from darkness to light, from death to immortality'.[72] And this passage is accomplished not only for Jesus but for all mankind. So Jesus says to his disciples: 'I go to prepare a place for you, that where I am there you may be also',[73] and he prays to the Father for them. 'I will that where I am, they also may be with me, that they may behold my glory.'[74] To behold the glory of God is to see the face of God, that is, to share in the divine being itself, to be 'one with the Father' just as the Son is, 'that they may be one, as Thou in me and I in thee, that they may be one in us'.[75]

VI

THE MYTH OF THE MESSIAH
AND HIS KINGDOM

A new creation, a new Paradise, a promised land, an Exodus or departure from this world – these were some of the images under which the destiny of mankind was pictured in the Bible. But the myth which took deepest root in Israel and which expressed above all the hopes and expectations of the people, was that of the Messiah and his kingdom. Israel had risen to the height of its greatness under David and his son Solomon, and a prophecy had been made that a son would be born to David by whom his kingdom should be established for ever. 'I will establish the throne of his kingdom for ever', it was said. 'I will be to him a father and he shall be my son.'[76] When this expectation was not realized under Solomon, and immediately afterwards the kingdom was divided between Israel and Judah, the promise of the Messiah, the 'anointed one', the King, who should establish the throne of David for ever, was projected into the future.

As the fortunes of Israel ebbed, the hope arose that God would finally intervene to overcome the enemies of Israel and set up the throne of David.[77] This Messianic King was seen as one who would rule over all the nations and destroy all his enemies, but at the same time he was hailed as a 'son of God': 'thou art my son, this day have I begotten thee,'[78] who should sit at the right hand of God: 'sit thou at my right hand until I make thy enemies thy footstool.'[79] He was also a priest-king like Melchizedek of old,[80] one who combined the royal and priestly office, the *sacerdotium* and *regnum*, 'Thou art a priest for ever of the order of Melchizedek.'[81] This figure of a warrior king, who is also a priest and a son of God, has haunted the imagination of Israel and is still a force in the world.

But there was another figure quite opposed to this, that of the Suffering Servant of Isaiah. When Israel was crushed beneath the feet of its enemies, the conception was born, not of a king who would conquer their enemies in war, but of one who would bear disgrace and shame and thereby atone for the sins of the people.[82] This 'suffering servant' is a figure of the people of Israel itself, which began to realize its vocation to conquer by suffering and endurance, a concept infinitely more profound than that of the warrior king, which has rarely been acknowledged, but which has inspired today the achievements of Mahatma Gandhi and Martin Luther King. This figure, though representative of the people as a whole, came to be focused also on the Messiah, and it was perhaps the greatest achievement of Jesus to have united these two figures in himself, that of the Messiah and the son of God with that of the suffering servant who lays down his life for his people, like the shepherd who lays down his life for the sheep.[83]

But finally there was another figure which attached itself

to that of the Messiah and influenced even more profoundly the mind of Jesus, that of the Son of Man. This figure appears first in the apocalypse of Daniel where the prophet sees 'one like to a son of man coming on the clouds of heaven'.[84] This marks a new stage in Israel's history, when the hope of a king like David was fading, and an intervention of God from above was expected. The apocalyptic writers look not so much for a transformation of the present world through a righteous king, but for an end to this world and the beginning of a 'new age' through the descent of a power from on high. This expectation was very strong in the time of Jesus and there is no doubt that he saw himself clearly figured in this Son of Man, when he said: 'you shall see the Son of Man, sitting at the right hand of power, and coming with the clouds of heaven.'[85] But the phrase 'son of man' (in Hebrew *Ben Enosh*) had also other meanings. It could be simply a paraphrase for 'man' as in Ezekiel[86] and in the Psalm: 'What is man that thou art mindful of him, and the son of man that thou visitest him.'[87] But the word 'man' itself was capable of an infinite richness of meaning. It could refer back to the first man, the Adam Kadmon, who is also the archetypal man, the Man created in the image of God. This links it with the Hindu Purusha,[88] who is also the primeval Man but at the same time the Cosmic Person, the Person in whom the whole creation is contained. This figure appears again in Islam as the Universal Man (*al-insan al Kamil*) of the Sufi mystics,[89] and again in the Dharmakaya, the cosmic body of the Buddha, or the Buddha nature which is in all men.[90]

There is no serious reason to doubt that Jesus used this term of himself. It was a phrase which could mean everything or nothing. It linked him with humanity as a whole as one of the 'sons of men', and at the same time opened up an infinite horizon, so that people were compelled to ask: 'who is this son of man?'[91] St Paul was only drawing out the implications of this phrase when he saw Christ as the second Adam. 'The first man was from the earth, earthy; the second Man is from heaven.'[92] And then he could go on to say: 'just as we have borne the image of the earthly man, so shall we also bear the image of the man from heaven.'[93] Thus the figure of the Messiah underwent a gradual transformation. From the warrior king who was to conquer his enemies and establish his throne by war, he came to be seen as the Suffering Servant who bears the sins of the people. From the son of God who sits in majesty on high, he came to be seen as the Son of Man, who shares the sufferings of mankind but triumphs over death and restores man to his original state as head of the creation. All these themes were woven together around the person of Jesus. He was seen first from one angle, then from another. He was the King of the house of David, but he was also the Suffering Servant of Isaiah. He was the Son of Man who had nowhere to lay his head;[94] but he was also the Son of God, who had ascended above the heavens, and was to come in glory in the clouds.[95] He was the priest who had entered into the heavenly sanctuary[96] and he was also the bridegroom who had prepared a marriage supper for his bride.[97]

As the myth of the Messiah was gradually built up round the figure of the son of David, who was to establish his kingdom, so the symbol of the kingdom underwent a similar transformation. It began as an earthly kingdom, a kingdom like that of David, in which Israel would triumph over all its enemies. Even in New Testament times there were Zealots, who wanted to restore the kingdom by force of arms, and the disciples of Jesus could ask, 'when will you restore the kingdom to Israel?'[98] and seek for places at his right hand and his left in the kingdom.[99]

Yet from the beginning this Kingdom was understood to be a kingdom in which the God of Israel would reign and the king would be his representative. Gradually all the implications of this came to be realized. One of the earliest Prophets, Micah, could speak of Jerusalem as a city to which the people of the world would go up, because 'the law of the Lord would go forth from Sion and the word of the Lord from Jerusalem,' and the result of this would be that 'they shall beat their swords into ploughshares and their spears into pruning hooks, nation shall not lift up sword against nation, neither shall they learn war any more'.[100] Here at one stroke we pass to a new idea of the kingdom. It is founded on the word or law of God and its effect is to abolish war and bring in the reign of peace. Isaiah the prophet has the same vision of the kingdom: 'Of the increase of his government and of peace there shall be no end, upon the throne of David and upon his kingdom, to establish it and to uphold it with judgement and righteousness for ever.'[101] The kingdom of the Messiah appears as a return to Paradise, when the spirit returns to man, the spirit of wisdom and understanding, of counsel and might, and of knowledge and the fear of the Lord, and the effect of this is to restore the law of righteousness, so as to bring justice to the poor and the weak, and finally to restore the original harmony between man and nature, so that 'the wolf shall dwell with the lamb and the leopard shall lie down with the kid, and the calf and the young lion and the fatling together, and a little child shall lead them'.[102]

The mythical character of the kingdom is here clearly established. It is no longer an earthly kingdom, but the reign of God on earth, when man and nature are restored to that 'original justice' for which they were created. This shows the stages in the growth of the myth of the kingdom. It is first of all the earthly kingdom of David established in Jerusalem, the holy city of Israel. Then it is seen as the ideal kingdom, restoring justice and peace between the peoples of the world and with the animal kingdom. Finally, in the book of Daniel, it appears as a heavenly kingdom, which is bestowed on the Son of Man. 'And there was given him dominion and glory and a kingdom, that all peoples and nations and languages should serve him: his dominion is an everlasting dominion, which shall not pass away and his kingdom that which shall not be destroyed'.[103] In the New Testament these three characteristics of the kingdom remain. It always has a basis in this world and yet it always has an ideal character, as a state of justice and peace to which humanity always aspires, and above all it has a 'heavenly' aspect; it is a manifestation of the eternal order, of the 'righteousness' of God himself, of man's communion with the infinite transcendent reality.

VII

THE MYTH OF THE NEW JERUSALEM AND THE CITY OF GOD

We have seen that Israel saw itself to be a nomad people, a people always journeying from place to place, and the journey through the desert was seen as a privileged time, when Israel felt itself to be under the special protection of God and received the law from his hands, which gave it an identity as a unique people. The city, on the other hand, represented by Babylon, was seen as a symbol of man's sinful state, alienated from God and setting his heart on the good things of this world. Still to this day the great city, whether London or New York or Tokyo, remains a symbol of 'this-worldliness', of the pursuit of wealth and power and pleasure, which takes man away from God. It was only after much hesitation that Israel was permitted to have a king[104] and to form a kingdom. This was seen as a sign that Israel would forsake God and 'serve other gods'.[105]

Again, when David wanted to build a temple for the Lord, it was pointed out that the God of Israel had always 'been moving about with a tent for his dwelling'[106] and it was left to his son Solomon to build the temple at Jerusalem. This focuses one of the fundamental problems of human existence. When a people settles in a land, it needs a law to govern it and a king or some ruler to administer the law. Again, when a religion is established, it needs an organization, a priesthood and a church or temple. Yet always the institution, whether of Church or State, tends to overshadow the Spirit which it is intended to serve. Thus the Law was given to Israel to regulate its civil and religious life, a priesthood and sacrifice was established and a magnificent temple was built. Yet all these things, though necessary for the functioning of religion, yet came to overshadow the religion itself and to be an obstacle to its growth.

It is the same with the Christian churches today. The early Church broke with the temple and priesthood and sacrifice of Israel, and developed a very simple life of worship and prayer of its own 'breaking bread in their homes'.[107] But very soon a new priesthood and sacrifice came into being; churches were built and the Church developed an elaborate organization. With the conversion of Constantine Christianity became the religion of the Empire, and the uneasy alliance of Church and State began, which has continued to the present day, sometimes the Church dominating the State, sometimes the State controlling the Church, and always a tension remaining between God and Caesar, Emperor and Pope, persecutor and persecuted. How can this tension be resolved? It would seem that there is no way to resolve it, as long as we remain in this world of dualities. Religion will always be corrupted by the pursuit of power and wealth, and the State will always use its power and wealth to suppress anything which might challenge its absolute authority. It is for this reason that a great many people today rebel against both Church and State. Religion is seen as belonging to the 'Establishment', the established order of power and wealth and prestige, and truth, it is felt, must be sought outside the Establishment. In the same way the State, whether capitalist or communist, is felt to be an inhuman order, often of built-in injustice, and liberation is to be sought in freedom from the tyranny of the law.

It seems to me that in the New Testament an answer was given to this problem of extraordinary depth, whose implications have not yet been realized. The Law – the Torah – was given by God to Moses. It laid down the law of religion and morality and of civil society in minute detail, and obedience to this law was considered to be the test of obedience to God. It was emphasized again and again that Israel's salvation would depend on the observance of the 'statutes and ordinances' of the law.[108] They were to be bound for a sign upon the head and for frontels before the eyes; to be written on the doorposts of the house and on the gate.[109] They were to be handed down from generation to generation and were to last 'for ever'.[110] Yet all this law was to pass away – the temple and the priesthood and the sacrifices and the solemn observances – and only circumcision and the Passover and a few other rites were to remain. In the New Testament this was to be the critical question – how much of the Jewish law was to be retained? Jesus himself prophesied the destruction of the temple, which took place forty years later in the year AD 70. But he had already changed the very basis of the law, when he declared that 'the

Sabbath was made for man, not man for the Sabbath; therefore the Son of Man is Lord of the Sabbath'.[111] At one stroke the law was relativized and the way was open to reducing the whole law to two commandments: to love God and to love one's neighbour.[112]

It was left to St Paul to work out all the implications of this. For him as a Jew, 'educated according to the strict manner of the Law',[113] the crucial question was, had a Christian to accept the law, to be circumcised and observe its precepts? Facing this problem led St Paul to see the law in a totally new light. The observances of the law were a 'pedagogue', a guide for mankind, when in a state of immaturity, like children in need of a master. He goes even further than this. The law is a sign of human sinfulness. People only need a law, a system of rules and regulations, because they are subject to their passions and desires. A person who has reached maturity discovers the law not as an external compulsion but as an interior principle.[114]

All the externals of religion, rituals and sacrifices, priesthood and temple, are external signs intended to awaken faith, to enable the person to pass from the external law of appearances to the inner law of the spirit. It is the same in all religions. Christianity itself soon came to develop a ritual and a sacrifice, a church and a priesthood, an organization of ever greater complexity. But this system of law is like every other system. It is conditioned by time and history, by external circumstances and events, and like all such systems it is destined to pass away. A visitor to Rome seeing the magnificent building of St Peter's might well be inclined to say, 'Look, Teacher, what wonderful stones and what wonderful buildings,' and be told, 'Do you see these great buildings? There will not be left one stone upon another that will not be thrown down.'[115] Such is the fate of all earthly religion.

This is the mystery of the new Jerusalem. Jerusalem was the city where David established his throne and Solomon built the temple, 'a house for the name of Yahweh, the God of Israel'.[116] The temple was burnt with fire by the Babylonians when Jerusalem was captured in 587 BC[117] and then rebuilt under Zerubbabel in 575 BC[118] and enlarged on a grand scale by Herod in 19 BC. It was this temple of Herod which was finally destroyed in AD 70.

Such is the story of the earthly temple. But behind this story is the myth of Jerusalem as the 'city of God'. Jerusalem is the 'holy mountain' on which God has set up his king.[119] It is the City of God, the holy mountain, 'beautiful in elevation, the joy of the whole earth'.[120] It is the 'perfection of beauty' from which God has shined forth.[121] Most striking of all, it is the city to which all the nations will come, recognizing her as their mother.[122] We have seen how Isaiah speaks of Israel as 'married' to God, and so Jerusalem is seen as 'a crown of beauty' and a 'royal diadem' in the hand of God.[123] Finally, Jerusalem is seen as a sign of the new creation: 'Behold, I create Jerusalem a rejoicing and her people a joy, and I will rejoice in Jerusalem and joy in my people.'[124]

In the light of this one can understand the sadness of Jesus in his lament over Jerusalem. 'O Jerusalem, Jerusalem, killing the prophets and stoning them who are sent to you, how often would I have gathered your children together as a hen gathers her brood under her wings, and you would not. Behold, your house is forsaken and desolate.'[125] But this marks clearly the breach with the earthly Jerusalem and it is made clear that 'neither on this mountain nor in Jerusalem shall you worship the Father . . . but the hour is coming and now is, when the true worshippers will worship the Father in spirit and truth.'[126] This worship 'in spirit and truth' marks the final liberation of man from temples and churches and mosques, and the final awakening to the eternal order of which they are the temporal signs. In the letter to the Hebrews this passage to the eternal order is made explicit when it says that Christ has entered into the 'true tabernacle' which is set up 'not by man but by God', of which the temple with its priesthood and sacrifice is only a 'copy and a shadow'.[127] For the true temple is 'not of this creation',[128] and Christ by his offering of himself, once for all, has put an end to the old priesthood and sacrifice. Finally, in the Revelation of St John, the seer sees the Holy City, the new Jerusalem 'coming down out of heaven from God, prepared as a bride adorned for her husband'.[129] Here the myth of the earthly Jerusalem is finally dissolved and Jerusalem is seen for what it is, a symbol of God's dwelling among men. 'Behold, the dwelling of God is with men. He will dwell with them and they shall be his people and God himself will be with them.'[130] It is significant that there is no temple in this heavenly city. 'I saw no temple in the city, for its temple is the Lord God, the Almighty and the Lamb. And the city has no need of sun or moon to shine upon it, for the glory of the Lord is its light, and its lamp is the Lamb.'[131] One is reminded of the great saying of the Upanishad: 'The sun shines not there nor the moon, nor the stars, nor lightning much less earthly fire. When he shines everything shines after him, and by his light all these are lighted.'[132]

Thus the new Jerusalem becomes a symbol of the new creation. Every human institution, every land or city or kingdom or temple or church is a 'copy or a shadow', a manifestation in time and space, of an eternal reality. The whole creation and all human history are 'symbols' of a transcendent mystery. All religious doctrines are 'myths' or symbolic expressions of a truth which cannot properly be expressed. Every form of priesthood and sacrifice, of ritual and sacrament, belongs to the world of 'signs' which is destined to pass away. Today, more than ever, we are being called to recognize the limitations of every form of religion. Whether Christian or Hindu or Buddhist or Muslim, every religion is conditioned by time and place and circumstances. All their outward forms are destined to pass away. As a Muslim saying has it: 'Everything passes save his face.'[133] But in all these outward forms of religion, of doctrine and sacrament and organization, the one eternal Truth is revealing itself, the one Mystery is making itself known, the one transcendent Being is making itself manifest. Idolatry consists in stopping at the sign; true religion is the passing through the sign to the Reality.

IV

The Christian Revelation:
the Rebirth of the Myth

I

THE WAY OF INTUITIVE WISDOM

I come back again to ask as I have done many times before, what has India taught me, and what has she to teach the world? It seems to me as to many others today that we are entering on a new age. The age of Western domination is over and the future of the world lies not in Western Europe and North America but in Asia, Africa and Latin America. This does not mean that we have to reject the Western heritage. The ideas of Western science and democracy have penetrated to every part of the world. The ideal of Western science, of the accurate observation of phenomena, of rational analysis, free from all partiality or emotional bias, of the discovery of the 'laws' of nature, that is regular patterns of events, and of their application for the benefit of mankind – these ideals remain of permanent value. So also the principles of democracy, of the value of the individual person, of the 'rights' of man, that is the right of each individual to life and growth and health and education, above all, the right of self-government in whatever political structure it may be expressed – it need hardly be said the right of woman to equality with man – these are marks of the growth of humanity to greater maturity, to a greater realization of what it means to be human.

But the limitations of Western science and democracy have become more and more evident. The disastrous effects of Western industrialism, physical, social and psychological, polluting the world and threatening to destroy it, are only too evident. But this is not an 'accident' due to the misuse of science and technology; it is due to a fundamental defect in Western man. By Western man, I mean of course, not simply people who live in Western Europe and North America, but the peculiar culture which derives originally from Socrates and the Greek philosophers and has in the course of time produced the typical Western man who is to be found all over the world today. Western science and democracy are an inheritance from the Greeks. For a long time, from the time of Christ till the Renaissance, this Greek culture under the direction of Rome permeated both Eastern and Western Europe and built up a unique culture, in which the genius of Greece and Rome blended with the oriental Semitic culture of the Christian religion to create a balanced and harmonious way of life, which has left its record in the architecture, the art, the poetry, the philosophy and theology of the Middle Ages. But at the Renaissance this harmony was lost, and the dominant, aggressive, masculine, rationalist mind of the West took charge, so that Europe remains today in a permanent state of imbalance.

The balance can only be restored when a meeting takes place between East and West. This meeting must take place at the deepest level of the human consciousness. It is an encounter ultimately between the two fundamental dimensions of human nature: the male and the female – the masculine, rational, active, dominating power of the mind, and the feminine, intuitive, passive and receptive power. Of course, these two dimensions exist in every human being and in every people and race. But for the past two thousand years, coming to a climax in the present century, the masculine, rational mind has gradually come to dominate Western Europe and has now spread its influence all over the world.

The Western world – and with it the rest of the world which has succumbed to its influence – has now to rediscover the power of the feminine, intuitive mind, which has largely shaped the cultures of Asia and Africa and of tribal people everywhere. This is a problem not only of the world as a whole, but also of religion. The Christian churches, Catholic, Orthodox, and Protestant, have all been shaped by the Western mind. They have built up structures of doctrine and discipline, of law and morality, which all bear the impress of the Western genius. The Eastern churches have retained something of an Oriental character but are still dominated by the Greek mind. Even the original Semitic tradition, which gave birth to Christianity, though deeply intuitive has still a dominantly masculine character. All the Christian churches, Eastern and Western, have to turn to the religions of the East, to Hinduism, Buddhism, Taoism and the subtle blend of all these in Oriental culture, and to the deep intuitions of tribal religion in Africa and elsewhere, if they are to recover their balance and evolve an authentic form of religion which will answer to the needs of the modern world.

What then do I mean by intuition as distinct from reason, by this feminine power of the mind? This is a question which has been with me from the time when I began to think at all for myself. I tried to answer it when I first began to study philosophy, in two essays on the Power of the Imagination and the Power of Intuition. Both these essays, it may be remarked, were rejected by Catholic periodicals at the time, because they were not sufficiently 'Thomistic'. And indeed, I felt at the time that this is the great weakness of the philosophy of St Thomas Aquinas, magnificent as it is in its own way, that it has no place for the power of intuition. It is true that St Thomas allows in a roundabout way for a power of knowledge by 'connaturality' or 'sympathy', an 'affective' knowledge, but it has very little place in his strictly rational system. For him, as for the Greeks and for modern Western man, knowledge is to be found in concepts and judgements, in logic and reason, in systematic thought. Western science, for all its concern with observation and experiment, remains firmly attached to this mode of thought and as such is an inheritance from Greek and scholastic philosophy.

What then is intuition? Intuition is a knowledge which derives not from observation and experiment or from concepts and reason but from the mind's reflection on itself. What distinguishes the human mind above everything else is not its powers of observation and experiment, which animals also possess in some degree, nor its power of logical and mathematical reasoning, which a computer can imitate quite successfully, but its power of self-reflection. The human mind is so structured that it is always present to itself. When I eat or even when I sleep, when I feel joy or sorrow, when I love or hate, I do not merely undergo a certain physical or psychological process. I am present to myself, and in a certain sense aware of myself, eating and sleeping, experiencing joy or sorrow, loving or hating. When I know something I know that I know, in other words, I know not only what I know, but also myself as knowing. Every human action or suffering is accompanied by a self-awareness, a reflection on the self. The difficulty is that this self-awareness, this self-reflection, is not conscious in the ordinary sense. It is often referred to as 'unconscious'. Jung has made us familiar with this concept of the knowledge of the unconscious underlying all conscious knowledge. But this is an unsatisfactory term, since there is a kind of consciousness in this state. It can be called 'sub-conscious', but this again suggests that it is not really a state of consciousness. It may be called 'subliminal', that is, beneath the threshold (*limen*) of consciousness. Maritain in his *Creative Intuition in Art and Poetry* speaks of it as 'beneath the sunlit surface' of the mind. This comes nearer to the truth. Intuition belongs not to the sunlit surface of the mind, but to the night and the darkness, to the moonlit world of dreams and images, before they emerge into rational consciousness.

Let us try to grasp this. When I am eating or sleeping, when I simply experience my physical being, there is a dim, obscure awareness of myself eating and sleeping. The baby who has just learned to suck its mother's breast or remains blissfully asleep, has already an obscure awareness of itself, which will ultimately grow into full self-consciousness. Even before birth the child in the womb is beginning to experience itself. The proof of this is that all these experiences remain indelibly impressed on the mind, that is the memory. Years afterwards a person may discover that the trauma of birth or the experience of neglect in infancy have permanently affected the psyche and can be brought back to mind. I have said that even in sleep there is an obscure self-awareness. This is obvious in dreams, but even in deep sleep which Hindus call *sushupti*, it is held that there is a self-awareness. The mind sinks back into its source and the memory of it remains. One can understand the difficulty of what we are attempting to do. We are trying to bring up into rational consciousness and to express in rational concepts what is beyond rational consciousness but which nevertheless leaves its mark on the rational mind.

Perhaps we could speak of the 'passive intellect'. There is

an active intellect, the *intellectus agens*, which abstracts rational concepts from our sense experience and develops scientific theories. But there is also a passive intellect. Before the intellect begins to act, it receives the impressions of the experience of the body, the senses, the feelings, the imagination. This is the source of intuition. All my experiences of my physical being, of my own body and of the world around me, of my emotional reactions and the images which they arouse in me, are impressed on the passive intellect. There is no such thing as a mere sensation, a mere feeling, a mere thought. Every sensation, every feeling, every imagination affects my mind, modifies my being. I live and act as a whole. However obscure this self-awareness may be, it is there in every action and in every sensation, in every thought and feeling. I am present to myself in every moment of my being. This is the very structure of my mind, of my consciousness. If I probe my consciousness sufficiently, I can become aware of this subliminal consciousness. I can go beneath the surface of my mind and explore its depths.

This is what has been taught in the West as a method of psycho-analysis, but the Western psychologist rarely goes beyond the level of the dream consciousness and that of repressed emotions, whereas in the East, in Hindu and Buddhist and Taoist yoga, they have penetrated to the depths of the psyche and discovered its original ground. This is what Western man has to learn to do. He has to find the path of self-realization which has been followed for centuries in the East.

The self is not the little conscious ego, constructing its logical systems and building its rational world. The self plunges deep into the past of humanity and of the whole creation. I bear within my mind, my memory in the deep sense, the whole world. The movement of atoms and molecules, which make up the cells of my body, are all registered in the passive intellect. The formation of my body in the womb of my mother in all its stages is all stored in my memory. Every impulse of love or hate, of fear or anger, of pleasure or pain, has left its mark on my mind. Nor am I limited to the experience of my own body and feelings. I am physically and psychologically linked with all the world around me. My body is the focus of electro-magnetic phenomena, of forces of gravitation and of all kinds of chemical changes. My feelings are reactions to a whole world of feelings both past and present in which I am involved. All this has left its impression on my mind. Well did Hamlet remark: 'What a piece of work is man!' My mind is an unfathomable mystery, reflecting the whole world, and making me a centre of consciousness among innumerable other such centres, each reflecting all.

Intuition, then, is the knowledge of the passive intellect, the self-awareness, which accompanies all action and all conscious, deliberate reflection. It is passive: it comes from the world around me, from the sensations of my body, from my feelings and spontaneous reactions. That is why intuition cannot be produced. It has to be allowed to happen. But that is just what the rational mind cannot endure. It wants to control everything. It is not prepared to be silent, to be still, to allow things to happen. Of course, there is a passivity of inertia, but this is an 'active passivity'. It is what the Chinese call *wu wei*, action in inaction. It is a state of receptivity. 'Let us open our leaves like a flower,' said Keats, 'and be passive and receptive.' These words inspired me at the very beginning of my journey, but it is only now that I realize their full significance. There is an activity of the mind which is grasping, achieving, dominating, but there is also an activity which is receptive, attentive, open to others. This is what we have to learn. The classical expression of this intuitive wisdom is to be found in the Tao Te Ching, which speaks of the Spirit of the Valley and the Mystic Female. 'The door of the Mystic Female,' it says, 'is the root of heaven and earth.' 'In opening and closing the Gates of Heaven can you play the part of the female? In comprehending all knowledge can you renounce the mind?' 'Attain to the utmost emptiness, hold firm the basis of Quietude.' 'To return to the root is repose.'[1] These are the principles which underlie the wisdom of the East, which the West has to discover and which China and the East have to recover if the world is to find its balance.

The passive intellect is the 'feeling intellect' of Wordsworth. It is the intellect united with feeling, with the emotions. It was thus that Wordsworth described poetry as 'emotion recollected in tranquillity'. It rises in the emotions and ascends to the level of the intellect, where it is 'recollected', gathered into unity and given meaning. Wordsworth described the whole process beautifully, when in the 'Lines written above Tintern Abbey' he spoke of sensations

> felt in the blood and felt along the heart
> and passing even into the purer mind
> with tranquil restoration.

This describes the whole process of intuitive knowledge. It is an integral knowledge embracing the whole man, starting from the 'blood', the physical being, passing through the heart, the seat of the affections, the psychic being, and finally reaching the 'purer mind', not the reason but the intellect, the intuitive mind.

Thus intuition exists at every level of our being. It starts with the 'blood', with bodily awareness. Even at this level the intellect, the self, is present. The idea of 'thinking with the blood' is not an illusion. There is a very profound self-awareness at this deepest level of our being. Tribal people, especially in Africa, always tend to think with the blood, expressing themselves in the beat of drums and the movements of the dance. This is an authentic mode of knowledge, of self-discovery and self-affirmation. All simple people tend to live more from their bodies than from their minds, that is, from the intuitive knowledge of the body rather than from the rational knowledge of the mind.

D. H. Lawrence, who was the prophet of this kind of knowledge, has expressed it well: 'We have lost almost entirely the great intrinsically developed sensual awareness or sense-awareness and sense-knowledge of the ancients. It was a great depth of knowledge, arrived at direct by instinct and intuition as we say, not by reason. It was a knowledge based not on words but on images. The abstraction was not into generalizations or into qualities but into symbols, and the connection was not logical but emotional.'[2] It must be emphasized that this is real knowledge: it is not merely sensual or emotional experience. It is sense awareness, emotional experience reflected in the mind, not in the rational mind, the abstract intelligence, but in the intuitive mind, the passive intellect. It finds expression not in abstract concepts but in concrete gestures, in images and symbols, in dance and song, in ritual sacrifice, in prayer and ecstasy.

It is the great illusion of the Western world that knowledge consists in abstract thought and that an illiterate person is ignorant. In reality, many illiterate people possess a wisdom which is totally beyond the reach of Western man. Ramakrishna, the Hindu saint, who more than anyone else was responsible for the renewal of Hinduism in the last century, was an illiterate Brahmin, who spoke from the depths of an intuitive wisdom.

Intuition, then, can exist at the level of bodily instinct. People who habitually go barefoot and expose their bodies to the sun, as they do in many parts of Asia and Africa, have an intuitive awareness of the power, the *sakti* in Hindu terms, in the earth, in the air, in the water and in the fire of the sun. They experience these forces of nature acting upon them and have an instinctive knowledge of the hidden powers of nature. A farmer often has an instinctive knowledge, a knowledge by sympathy, of the productive powers of the earth, of the effects of the seasons of the year, and the changes of the moon, and of the weather reflected in the sky. Rational scientific knowledge can increase the precision of this kind of knowledge and make it systematic, but it alienates man from nature and creates an artificial world.

People who live in a world of concrete roads and buildings, of steel structures and plastic instruments, lose touch with the world of spontaneous feeling and imaginative thought. This is because the rational, scientific mind separates itself from the 'feeling intellect', the source of intuitive wisdom. It is not that science and reason are wrong in themselves, but that they are divorced from sense and feeling. What we have to seek is the 'marriage' of reason and intuition, of the male and the female, then only shall we discover a human technology corresponding with man's deepest needs.

The first level of intuition, then, is on the physical level. This includes, of course, the sphere of sex. Sex itself is a means of knowledge. It is significant that the Hebrew speaks of a man 'knowing' a woman in marriage: 'Adam knew his wife, Eve, and she conceived.'[3] Let us remember in passing that by a reverse process knowledge is spoken of in terms of sex. A 'concept' is something 'conceived' by the mind, a fruit of the union between the mind and nature, between *purusha* and *prakriti* in Hindu terms.

Again, we must remember that sex in a human being is
never a merely physical process. It involves the body, the
feelings, the affections. It is 'felt in the blood and felt along the
heart', to apply the language of Wordsworth, and 'passes
even into the purer mind'. It touches the depths of human
consciousness awakening the intuitive powers of the mind
and transforming the self. A man knows a woman in sexual
union with a knowledge deeper than any science or
philosophy. This is the wisdom by which most people live, a
wisdom of human intimacy and affection, engaging the
whole person. But this union takes place at three levels. There
is first the level of the physical senses, of the blood and the
nerves and the resulting orgasm, and this is already a kind of
knowledge. The self is present in this experience; it is already
a specifically human experience. But deeper than the physical
intimacy is the emotional union. There is a craving for
warmth, for closeness, for intimacy in every human being.
The first impulse of the baby is for the warmth and intimacy
of the mother's breast. But behind this desire for warmth and
intimacy there is a desire for love, for emotional satisfaction.
The intimacy desired is not merely physical but psychological. In sexual union also it is not merely the physical
intimacy which is sought but a sharing of love, a self-giving,
a communion, in which each enriches the being of the other.
This again is a form of knowledge, a knowledge of love, of
communion, in which each discovers the other.[4]

In this union of love the man learns to know the woman
and the woman learns to know the man, they mutually
discover their own masculinity and femininity. This goes far
beyond a merely emotional state. It is an awakening to the
self. Each discovers a new aspect of his and her self. In every
sexual union this self-knowledge is present, but when the
emotional union is superficial, self-knowledge remains

latent. It is only when the emotional union is deep and lasting that self-knowledge can grow. When this takes place a new level of knowledge is reached. It is no longer a merely physical or emotional intuition, it is a growth in personal knowledge, an awakening to the inner self. Like every intuition it is a reflection of the self on the self, a self-presence, but here the self discovers a new dimension of its being. The passive intellect, the inner vision is awakened to a new level of understanding. In a really profound union of love this may pass into a state of ecstasy. The self goes beyond itself and awakens to the ground of its being in self-transcendence. Then man and woman go beyond the duality of sex and discover their oneness in a love which is total fulfilment.

It is important to realize that all sexual love tends towards this transcendent state. No man or woman can be finally satisfied with a physical or emotional union. Love goes beyond the body and the feelings and reaches to the depth of the human being, where the division of male and female no longer exists. The man and the woman find the totality of their being; in each the male and the female are united, and the division of human nature is overcome. This is the supreme intuition of the self, which is found in the great mystics. It is no accident that the mystical experience is so often described in terms of sexual union. This is not a 'sublimation' in the Freudian sense. It is an opening of human nature to the full dimension of its being. It is of the very nature of human love that it cannot be satisfied with physical contact or emotional sympathy. It seeks a radical fulfilment in total self-giving. For some, sexual union may be the way to this total self-giving and self-discovery; others may awaken to this ecstasy of love in the presence of nature like Wordsworth; others may find it in loving service and self-sacrifice. But whatever the way, this ecstasy of love leads to the supreme wisdom, to the discovery of the depth of the self, no longer in isolation, but in the communion of love, for which it was created.

There is, then, a sphere of physical, biological intuition and of emotional, affective intuition. But beyond these there is the sphere of imaginative intuition. It is here that the intuitive power of the mind is most clearly manifest. The experiences of the body with its sensations and emotions are all reflected in the imagination. The imagination is primarily a passive power – it reflects the images of the world around us and of our own internal experiences. It is the sphere of what Jung called the archetypes. Human experience is structured round certain primordial images – the father, the mother, the child, the bride, the bridegroom, the water and the fire, the shadow and the darkness – these are all archetypal images in what Jung called the 'unconscious', but which I would call the subliminal depths of consciousness. For these archetypes are all forms of intuition; they are images reflecting the self, rising in the depth of self-consciousness. In most people these archetypes are hidden, they have not come up into the light of reflective consciousness. But in the poet and artist, the archetypes emerge into the light of consciousness. The passive intellect receives these images from the depths of its physical and emotional experience and sheds on them the light of intelligence. This is when the intuition begins to emerge from the darkness of physical and emotional experience into the clear light of knowledge.

But this knowledge is not a rational, abstract, conceptual knowledge. The mind does not 'abstract' (draw out) from the experience of the body to form a concept and to reason from it. The intellect illumines the actual concrete experience, penetrates into the physical and emotional world and fills it with light. Not only poets but most people in a normal society live from the imagination rather than from abstract reason. It is only the artificial world of Western man that seeks to educate everyone in habits of abstract thought and creates logical systems, expressed in the jargon of the scientific mind.

In a normal human society, such as still exists in a large part of Asia and Africa, man lives by the imagination and expresses himself in the language of the imagination, in gestures and rituals, in speech consisting of symbols, which reflect the self and the world in concrete images often accompanied by music and dance. But, of course, it is in the great poets and artists that we can see the full development of the human imagination. They bring to perfection what in most people is obscure and inchoate, but it is because they draw on a basic human faculty common to all men, that the great poets speak to all men. Homer and the Greek tragedians, Virgil and Dante, Shakespeare and Goethe all speak this universal human language and it is to them that we go for the deepest understanding of human nature. In the same way, it is to the great novelists like Tolstoy and Dostoyevsky, with their imaginative insight, that we look for the deepest understanding of our human condition today.

What therefore is the poetic imagination? Maritain[5] has defined it as 'the intercommunion between the inner being of things and the inner being of the human self'. There is, as we have seen, a presence of the self in every human experience, but in most people this presence is only half realized, or not at all. In the poet this self-presence becomes conscious, the latent self-awareness grows into a conscious awareness through his experience of the world around him. He is more than usually sensitive to the world of the senses, to sight and sound and touch and taste and smell, and these sensations with their accompanying images enter deep into his consciousness. They are reflected in the depth of his being, in the passive intellect, and become intuitive. That is, the intellect penetrates into the depth of his self-consciousness and draws forth the images in it, which focus his experience. The world is reflected in his imagination in all its concrete richness, where feeling and thought are fused together.

The abstract rational mind creates a world of concepts, separated from concrete reality, but the imaginative mind re-creates the concrete world, reflecting it in symbols, whether of words or of rhythmical movements or of painted signs or of architectural forms. All genuine art springs from this profound experience of the self in the world and the world in the self. It is a primordial human experience, from which language itself and every form of self-expression emerges. It is the neglect of this world of the imagination, of 'art' in the deepest and widest sense, in favour of a world of reason dominated by 'science', that has caused the imbalance of Western civilization. This does not mean that science and reason are wrong in themselves. They are essential elements in human nature, and the development of these faculties in the West from the time of the Greeks is an essential element in human progress. But the domination of science and reason, and the practical suppression of art and imagination in normal education, has caused a fundamental imbalance in Western culture.

This is but one aspect of the domination of man over woman, of the aggressive male intellect over the feminine, intuitive imagination, which has affected all Western culture. It is typical of this outlook that it thinks that man and woman only differ physically and that the different races only differ in their colour. It does not recognize the profound, psychological difference between man and woman and between Asian, African and European man. This is due to blindness to the feminine aspect in human nature. Every man and woman is both male and female, and in every person the marriage of the male and the female has to take place. When man refuses to recognize the feminine aspect in himself, he despises or exploits woman and exalts reason over intuition, science over art, man over nature, the white races with their dominant reason over the coloured peoples with their intuitive feeling and imagination. This has been the course of Western civilization over the past centuries. Now we are awakening to the place of woman in society, to the meaning of sex and marriage, to the value of art and intuition and to the place of the coloured peoples in the civilization of the world. What has to take place is a 'marriage' of East and West, of the intuitive mind with the scientific reason. The values of the scientific mind must not be lost, but they need to be integrated in the wider vision of the intuitive mind.

Both reason and intuition by themselves are defective, just as man is defective without woman, woman without man. Intuition by itself is blind. It is an obscure awareness of the self in the experience of the world. The intuition easily becomes swamped by the emotions. This is the negative aspect of woman, the source of fickleness and instability, the *femina mutabile semper* of Virgil. It creates the image of the wanton, the temptress, the scarlet woman. It is the source of credulity and superstition, of witchcraft and sorcery, of vagueness and confusion of thought. The growth of science and reason in the West was largely a reaction against this unbalanced intuition, seen in the superstitions of the medieval Church, the cult of witchcraft and sorcery, and religious fanaticism. Yet the answer to this was not the rejection of the intuitive mind, but its marriage with the rational mind. Intuition begins in the darkness of the child in the womb. It grows through the awakening of emotional and imaginative experience, but it eventually has to be drawn up through the passive intellect, on which all this experience of the senses and the emotions is impressed, into the clear light of the mind. It is then that the marriage of imagination and reason, of the active and passive intellect, takes place. It is this that we see in the great poets. In them the deep experience of physical being and the riches of emotional and imaginative life are informed by reason.

Reason itself, the active intellect, is taken up into the intuitive mind, that is, into the reflective knowledge of the self, and reason itself becomes intuitive. It is this that we find in Dante. He draws on the depth of human passion and sensitivity, goes through all the emotions of love and hate, of hope and despair, of joy and sorrow, and embodies all this profound experience in a vast imaginative vision. All this comes out in the sound and melody, the rhyme and rhythm, the verbal richness and concrete imagery of his verse. But with all this there is a skeleton of hard reason, of subtle philosophy and theology, of doctrine and argument. Yet this skeleton of abstract thought is integrated in the imaginative vision of the whole. Philosophy and theology have been made into poetry, and the intuitive power of the mind has assimilated all these diverse elements into itself.

But even with Dante we have not yet reached the culmination of the intuitive mind. The poet synthesizes all these elements of human experience into a unitive vision, but he remains dependent on images and concepts. There is a further vision which goes beyond images and concepts, as Dante himself experienced when in the culminating vision of the *Paradiso* he said:

Henceforth my vision mounted to a height
Where speech is vanquished and must lag behind.[6]

There is a point where intuition, having passed through the realms of darkness and of twilight into the Sun, now passes beyond. It carries with it all the deep experience of the body and the blood, and all that the emotions and the imagination have impressed upon it, and now passing beyond images and thoughts, it 'returns upon itself' in a pure act of self-reflection, of self-knowledge. This is the experience of the mystic, who, set free from all the limitations both of body and of soul, enters into the pure joy of the spirit. The spirit is the culminating point of body and of soul, where the individual person transcends himself and awakens to the eternal ground of his being. The obscure intuition of physical being, the broadening intuition of emotional and imaginative experience, the light of reason discovering the laws and principles of nature and of man, all these are reflections of the pure light of intuition, in which the soul knows itself, not merely in its living relation with the world around or with other human beings, but in its eternal ground, the source of its being. At this point of the spirit the soul becomes self-luminous, or rather it discovers that it is itself but the reflection of a light which shines forever beyond the darkness, a light which is ever the same, pure, transparent, penetrating the whole creation, enlightening every human being, yet remaining ever in itself, tranquil and unchanged, receiving everything into itself and converting all into the substance of its own infinite being.

It is the discovery of this infinite, eternal, unchanging being, beyond the flux of time and change, beyond birth and death, beyond thought and feeling, yet answering to the deepest need of every human being, which is the goal of all religion and of all humanity. Here there is no longer a division between man and woman, for male and female are one. Here there is no longer a division between man and nature, for nature and man have found their unity in their source. Here there is no longer a division between classes and races and religions for here all have found the truth and the life for which they were seeking.

Yet this Being is not remote from any one or any thing. It is in each person and each thing as the ground of its own unique and individual being. The whole creation is grounded in this one Being; every atom and electron, every living cell and organism, every plant and animal, every human being, exists for ever in this eternal being. Time and change, body and soul, life and death veil this one reality, yet they themselves are its manifestations and exist in it. As an ancient saying has it: 'Everything that is there is here, everything that is here is there.' The world of time and space is a reflection of this eternal world; as Plato said: 'Time is a moving image of eternity'. All that takes place in time is seen and known in that eternal being. We are conditioned by time so that we see one thing after another and can never grasp the whole. But the intuitive vision is a vision of the whole. The rational mind goes from point to point and comes to a conclusion: the intuitive mind grasps the whole in all its parts. It is of this intuitive power of the mind that Eckhart said: 'This power has nothing in common with anything else, it knows no yesterday or day before, no morrow or day after (for in eternity there is no yesterday or morrow); there is only a present now; the happenings of a thousand years ago, a thousand years to come, are there in the present and the antipodes the same as here.'[7]

It is difficult for us with our time-bound minds and space-bound bodies to understand this eternal reality, or rather it is impossible, but that there exists in each one of us something that corresponds to that eternal being, a little spark, a ray of light, which touches our minds and awakens us to this transcendent mystery. The little spark is present in every human being, but for many it is totally hidden, for others it is kindled only occasionally, so that they get glimpses of that other world. It is only the mystic who penetrates beyond and sees the light, and even for him it is rarely that he can remain for long in such a state. It is only after death that we shall finally pass beyond the shadows and the darkness and see all things and all persons as they really are, in their eternal truth and their infinite reality.

It is the purpose of every genuine religion to reveal this transcendent mystery and to teach the way to its attainment. But this revelation is given not to the rational but to the intuitive mind, and the way to discover it is not by argument but by self-surrender, the opening of the self to its eternal ground. 'Not by the scriptures, not by the intellect, not by much study is this Self to be known. He whom the Self chooses by him the Self is attained.'[8] When we penetrate beyond the rational mind, we come upon a deeper self, a self that takes hold of our whole being, body and soul, and draws us into its infinite being.

But words here are inadequate, they stumble and fall. I am using abstract nouns like being, truth, reality, infinity, eternity. Each in its way points beyond our present mode of existence and directs the mind to that which is beyond the mind. But the words are of value only in so far as they awaken the little spark of intuition, and enable us to 'see into' the truth. That is why this knowledge cannot be attained by learning, it cannot be produced. We have to allow ourselves to be transformed, to become 'passive', but with a passivity that is infinitely receptive. There is a parallel between the original darkness of the mind, the state of 'deep sleep', what the Chinese call 'the uncarved block', where everything is potential waiting to receive the light, and this final state of total receptivity. The difference is that the potentiality of matter is conditioned; it has to go through various stages of evolution before it can be capable of life; and again life has to go through many phases of development before it can become conscious; so finally consciousness has to develop through sense, through feeling, through the imagination, through reason before it can become fully conscious of that being which is the source of matter, of life and of consciousness. But the hidden germ of intuition, of receptivity was present from the beginning, and the ultimate mystical experience is only the flower of that intuition which was hidden in the root of matter.

It is here that we can see the place of myth in human evolution. A myth is an expression of the intuitive mind. At first the mind may be almost totally absorbed in matter, in the body. The expression will be in bodily movements, in ritual and dance and the beating of drums. But this will be accompanied by deep feelings, an emotional involvement in the rhythm of nature, of earth and plants and animals, of sun and moon and sky, and this may be symbolized in some concrete object, a stone, a tree, an animal totem. But already there is a stirring of the imagination, of archetypal images from the depths of the unconscious, structuring the universe and giving it meaning. And behind all this the intuition is at work, a self-awareness, inchoate at first but growing with every contact with the external world, and building up the myth as the expression of this totality of experience, structuring the universe around the self. This self-awareness will at first be not so much individual as social, and not merely social but cosmic, an awareness of the self in its interdependence and intercommunion with the cosmic mystery. One can understand, therefore, how the myth embraces the totality of existence, giving man a place in the universe and organizing every aspect of his life.

Now myth is the source of all religion. One can see it at work in the most advanced as in the most primitive religions. In Greek religion one can see the evolution of the myth in the clearest way. Homer still lives in a mythological world, and the marvel of his poetry is that of the rational mind awaking to the world of myth and giving it an imperishable expression in a language which is rich and concrete, drawing on the depths of human experience, and structuring it in the light of a pure intelligence and giving it an ineffable beauty and grace. In Aeschylus the myth acquires a deep religious and moral meaning and the drama remains essentially that of a mythological world. In Sophocles the myth is still meaningful but it is the human drama which holds the centre of the stage. In Euripides, the 'rationalist', as Gilbert Murray called him, the myth has begun to lose its power and scepticism is taking its place.

From the time of Socrates myth gives way to reason and survives only as a background to poetry, while science and reason gradually take its place. This was a long process and it is only in the last hundred years that science and reason have come to dominate the world and the myth has died. Yet this is exactly our problem. Man cannot live without myth; reason cannot live without the imagination. It creates a desert, without and within. It becomes the sword of destruction, bringing death wherever it goes, dividing man from nature, the individual from society, woman from man, and man and woman from God. This is what the triumph of reason has done, and now we have to go back and recover the myth, return to the source, rediscover our roots, restore the wholeness to man and creation. The myth has to be reborn.

II

THE MYTH OF CHRIST

The two most powerful myths in the world today are those of Hinduism and Christianity. Hinduism still lives in the world of myth. Every Hindu child is given the name of a god or a goddess. The people flock in hundreds of thousands to the temples and places of pilgrimage. The festivals of the gods are still the great events of the year. Astrology rules people's lives and no matter of importance is undertaken without determining the auspicious time. Yet, at the same time, science and reason are spreading everywhere. All education is a secular education on Western lines, and the cinema, though it may retell the stories of the great myths, still spreads the values of Western man and is itself a typical product of Western technology.

How can the myth survive, or must India also succumb to the forces of Western civilization? Perhaps it is here that the future of the world will be decided. For at the heart of the mythology of Hinduism there is a philosophical tradition, a spiritual wisdom, far beyond that of the Greeks. There is nothing in Homer and the Greek tragedians to be compared with the spiritual depth of the Vedic tradition. While the Greek gods have faded away into poetic fictions, the Hindu gods have retained their power, because they have a deep, spiritual foundation. A series of great reformers from Ram Mohan Roy at the beginning of the last century, through Ramakrishna, Vivekananda, Rabindranath Tagore, Sri Aurobindo and Mahatma Gandhi, have restored Hinduism at every level, moral and spiritual, intellectual and poetic, philosophical and practical. Hinduism has faced the challenge of the Western world, and is attempting a synthesis of Western science and philosophy with its own cultural tradition.

This Hindu renaissance is something deeply significant for the whole world. Hindu gurus and teachers have gone with their message to all parts of the world, including Russia and other atheistic countries, and Western youth comes in thousands every year to India to learn the secrets of yoga and meditation. What is the secret of this Hindu wisdom, what is the meaning of the Hindu myth? Of course, there are many elements in the myth, as in all myths, which are merely fanciful (what Coleridge called 'fancy' as distinct from imagination). There are innumerable stories in the epics and *puranas* which no educated Hindu would take seriously. But the great figures of the myth, Vishnu and Siva, and the great Mother, the Devi, Rama and Krishna, even lesser figures like Ganesh, the elephant god, and Hanuman, the monkey god, are all deeply significant. They are all symbols of ultimate realities.[9] Vishnu, the Pervader, the Power that sustains the universe, the source of light, of life, of knowledge and of grace; Siva, the Destroyer, who brings to an end earthly existence, but leads to life beyond this world, the cosmic Dancer, who creates and dissolves the universe, the Lord of knowledge which transcends this world – these are figures of universal significance, insights into the ultimate nature of reality.

While Vishnu and Siva belong to the Cosmic myth, Rama and Krishna are legendary heroes; they are semi-historical figures which are seen to embody the ideal of humanity and to reveal God in man. They are incarnations (*avataras*) of Vishnu, manifestations of the infinite, timeless being in the world of space and time. As such they have, together with their consorts Sita and Radha, moulded the character of

Hindu men and women through the ages and been recognized not only as models of an ideal humanity but also as bestowers of grace on their worshippers. Even Ganesh, the elephant God, transcends all natural symbolism and is given a deep metaphysical meaning as a symbol of the union not merely of man with the animal world, but of man and God, and Hanuman, the monkey god, is seen as the perfect devotee, the incarnation of *bhakti*, of devoted love. Thus in Hinduism the myth is given metaphysical meaning and this in turn leads to the ultimate mystical reality. As we have seen, Brahman, Atman and Purusha, rising from the mythological ground of the Vedas, become symbols of ultimate reality, Being, consciousness and Bliss (*Saccidananda*), truth (*Satyam*), knowledge (*Jnanam*) and infinity (*Ananta*), but also personal being, wisdom and love (*Prema*).

What holds Hinduism together with its bewildering variety of gods and goddesses, of castes and sects, of doctrines and philosophies, of ways of prayer and meditation, of worship and devotion, is ultimately this mystical experience coming to birth in the Vedas, flowering in the Upanishads and bearing fruit in innumerable saints and sages and devotees, in poetry and music, art and philosophy, dance and ritual down to the present day. Of course, this Hindu myth is now constantly threatened by the destructive forces of Western civilization, and with that the mystical experience which is sustained by the myth is endangered.

Can the Hindu myth survive, can it be reborn, so as to offer to modern man the mystical experience, in which alone humanity can be fulfilled? It would seem that Hinduism, like every other religion, will have to undergo a process of 'de-mythologization'. All that is fanciful and no longer meaningful will have to be removed and the ancient symbols interpreted in the light of modern man's experience of the world. But this cannot be the work of 'reason', of learning and scholarship; it has to grow out of a mystical experience, in which the primordial meaning of the ancient symbols is recovered and their relevance to the world today is discerned. It is this process of 'de-mythologization' and re-interpretation in the light of a profound mystical experience which each religion has to undergo.

What of the Christian myth, how is that to be interpreted? We have seen that Christianity, no less than Hinduism, is based on a mythology – the myth of Creation and the Fall, of Paradise and the Promised Land, the Messiah and his Kingdom. In the New Testament the myth becomes crystallized in the person of Christ, his virgin birth, his death and resurrection, his ascension into heaven and his return in glory. All this is clearly the language of mythology. There are stories of virgin birth (as of the Buddha), of death and resurrection (as of Attis and Osiris), of ascents into heaven (as of the Pharaoh in Egyptian tradition), coming from all parts of the world. What is distinctive in the Christian myth? The Christian myth derives from the Hebrew tradition, and what distinguishes this tradition is its historical character. The Hindu myth is essentially a cosmic myth and belongs to the cosmic revelation. It is based on a cyclic view of time. As in nature everything goes in cycles, the sun rises and sets, the moon waxes and wanes, spring is followed by summer and autumn and winter and then returns again, so in the Hindu myth man is born and dies and is born again; God descends as an *avatara* again and again, 'when the righteousness declines and unrighteousness prevails';[10] the world comes forth from Brahman and returns at the dissolution (*pralaya*) only to come forth again.

Against this cyclic view of time the Hebrew tradition has a 'linear' view of time. Everything comes forth from God and moves according to a divine plan, towards an 'end', an *eschaton*. God reveals himself not only in nature but also in history, in the destiny of a particular people. He chooses Abraham and promises him that he shall become a great people. He calls Moses to deliver this people out of Egypt. He makes David a king over this people and promises him a son, who shall reign over his people for ever. This is the context of the myth of Christ. It is what may be called a historical myth, a myth that is rooted in historic time. Rama and Krishna are semi-historical figures, but they belong to the world of cyclic time, of the *avatara*, in whom God reveals himself from time to time. Even the Buddha, who is a genuine historical person, is included by Hindus among the *avataras*, and for Buddhists Sakyamuni is one of many Buddhas who have appeared in this world.

In all this there is no finality. The whole world process in which the *avataras* figure is a process of passing time. It belongs to the world of time and change which is passing away. It is a *maya*, neither real nor unreal (neither *sat* nor *asat*), an appearance of reality which has no ultimate meaning or purpose. It is like a dream, which has reality as long as it lasts, but disappears on waking. It is, in the famous analogy, like rope which is mistaken for a snake in the dark; when the light comes only the rope remains. So at the end of this world everything is dissolved and returns to its original state. Only the one, eternal, never-changing reality remains, which is Being, Knowledge and Bliss (*Saccidananda*), pure being in perfect consciousness of unending bliss. Such is the Hindu myth. In contrast with this the Hebrew myth is rooted in time. It is the story of a world 'created' by God, given its own being and consistency. It is the story of a people entering the stage of history, established in a definite land and coming to a head in a historic person and a historic event.

It is of the essence of Christian faith that Jesus of Nazareth was 'crucified under Pontius Pilate'. This is enshrined in the earliest Christian creed and is a fact of history known to the Roman historian Tacitus. This setting in concrete historical time is of the essence of the Christian revelation.

Hindu religion on the other hand has very little sense of historic time. It is called the *Sanatana Dharma*, the eternal religion. It has no beginning or end. It is the primordial religion, the universal, cosmic revelation, not tied to history in any way. Of course, the particular character of Hindu religion, the forms of its gods and goddesses, the language of the scripture, the structures of its temples and worship, the organization of its society, is determined by historic circumstances. But these have no ultimate significance. They are the passing forms and structures, in which the divine mystery has manifested itself; they will pass away, but the divine mystery, the eternal *Saccidananda*, which constitutes the essence of Hindu religion, will never pass away.

How can we reconcile these two 'myths', these two 'revelations' – the cosmic revelation of the infinite, timeless being manifesting in this world of time and change, but ultimately unaffected by it, with the Christian revelation of God's action in history, of the one, eternal Being acting in time and history and bringing this world of time and change into union with himself? This, it seems to me, is the problem of the modern world; on this depends the union of East and West and the future of humanity. We must try to see the values in each of these revelations, to distinguish their differences and to discover their harmony, going beyond the differences in an experience of 'non-duality', of transcendence of all dualities.

I think that we have to begin with the mystical experience which underlies both the Hindu and the Christian tradition. I have in the first part of this book described how I understand this Hindu mystical experience. It is an experience of absolute Being, absolute Knowledge and absolute Bliss. When I say 'absolute', I mean free from all limitations. Being, Reality (*sat*), is experienced as beyond all limitations of time and space, beyond word and thought, that is beyond all physical and psychological states of being. It is total transcendence, 'one without a second', 'not this, not this'. Of the validity of this experience there can be no doubt. Though it can never be described it is indicated in similar terms by Buddhist and Taoist, and Sufi mystics, by Plato and Plotinus and by the great Christian mystics. Here no difference arises. In every great religious tradition this absolute transcendence is seen as the goal, as the final answer to all man's questioning. But the question remains, what is the relation of this world, the physical world presented to our senses, and the psychological world of human sin and suffering, of good and evil, of knowledge and ignorance, of joy and sorrow, of love and hate, of beauty and ugliness, of time and change, to that final state? It is here that the differences arise. In the Hindu view, it would seem that these things have no ultimate value. They are all destined to pass away. 'The one remains, the many change and pass,' as Shelley put it, echoing the Platonic tradition. But in the Christian tradition each person, each thing, every event in space and time, has an infinite and eternal value. In the final state of timeless being, time is not abolished but fulfilled.

This is because the Christian mystical experience starts from a different point of view. It does not spring from the contemplation of the cosmos and the human soul, that is, from the basic human experience of the physical and psychological world, but from a specific historical event. The Christian mystical experience springs from the contemplation of the life and death of Jesus of Nazareth. Just as the Hindu myth grew out of the mystical experience of the Vedic seers and the saints and sages of India, so the Christian myth grew out of the experience of the disciples of Jesus at Pentecost, which is continually renewed in the saints and disciples of Christ throughout the ages. At Pentecost the disciples were 'filled with the Holy Spirit'.[11] They underwent a radical transformation. Something happened which transformed them from a group of weak and spiritless men, into a community of believers who set out to change the world. This something was a mystical experience. It was a breakthrough beyond time and change, beyond the agony of suffering and death which they had experienced in the crucifixion, into the world of absolute reality, which was summed up for the Hebrew in the name of God. They experienced God; they 'realized Brahman', as a Hindu would say, they 'Knew the Self', the Spirit, the eternal Truth, dwelling in the heart. They 'spoke with tongues',[12] interpreting this eternal truth in words of men. But this eternal word or Truth came to them through Christ. It was in Jesus of Nazareth, the man whom they had loved, whose death on the Cross they had witnessed, that this Truth was revealed to them. This is what is specific in the Christian mystical experience. The absolute reality is experienced as revealed in Christ, in the life and death of Jesus of Nazareth. It is not an experience of absolute reality revealed in the Cosmos, in the cycle of time in nature, nor in the human Self, the psychic being with its capacity for self-transcendence, but in a historic person and a historic event.

Yet when we have said this, we have surely shown that these two modes of experience, the cosmic and psychological on the one hand, and the personal and historical on the other, are not opposed but complementary. There is only one

Reality, one Truth, whether it is known through the experience of the cosmos and the human soul or through the encounter with a historic event. Moreover, the historic event cannot be separated from its place in the cosmos. Human history is part of cosmic history and Jesus as a historic person takes his place in the evolution of humanity. Again a historic event is encountered as part of our psychological experience; history is not merely a succession of events, but a succession of events interpreted in the light of human experience. Nor if Christian revelation centres on a historic person and a historic event can we deny that history also has its place in Hindu experience. Rama and Krishna may not be fully historical and their importance may not lie in their place in the context of human history, yet for the Hindu there is a revelation of God in the person of Rama and Krishna, and the events of their lives are 'revelatory', they awaken the soul to the experience of the divine, of absolute reality. What is significant in the life and death of Jesus is that it is seen in the context not of cyclic time, the 'eternal return' of the cosmic revelation, but in the context of the history of a particular people, and that it comes at the 'end' to 'give history its fulfilment'.[13] It is a unique historic event which gives meaning to all human history and reveals its final purpose.

What is required surely is that we should see these two 'revelations' in relation to one another. The danger of Hinduism is that it tends to see time and history as a passing phenomenon without any ultimate significance. The danger of Christianity is that it tends to attach too much importance to temporal events and to lose the sense of the timeless reality. The Hebrew had practically no sense of timeless reality. The whole of the Bible is set in the context of historic time – even the creation is seen as a temporal event: it used to be dated even as taking place in 4004 BC. So also the end of the world is seen as an event in time, just as infinity was conceived as an endless extent of space. The Hindu genius broke through this barrier of space and time, and saw infinity and eternity as states of being beyond the phenomenal world in which reality is experienced in pure consciousness without any limitation.

How can we reconcile these two points of view? The Hindu surely needs to discover the real value of time and history. In the context of the modern world, when India is awakening to its destiny as a nation, a philosophy which denies the value of progress and development in time and history will never answer the need of the people. Liberation is not to be found only by taking refuge in temples and holy places but by building up a nation in justice and charity. But the Christian also must learn that the Kingdom of God is not to be found in this world, however important the work of the world and the service of man may be. The Kingdom of God lies beyond history in the timeless reality in which all things find their fulfilment. In the Hebrew context this was expressed in terms of the beginning of a 'new age'. The age (the *aion*) of this world, it was declared, had passed, and a new age had begun.[14] This was the age to which the prophets had looked forward, the Day of the Lord, when God would intervene and bring to an end this evil world and inaugurate the Kingdom of God. It was the experience of the disciples of Christ at Pentecost which gave rise to this belief. This was an experience of 'God', that is of absolute reality, but this experience had inevitably to be expressed in terms of the mythology of the Old Testament. As we have seen, myth is the language of imaginative insight into ultimate reality. In no other way could the disciples of Christ express themselves but in the language of the Old Testament, the myth which had shaped their minds and their attitude to life.

The first way, therefore, in which they expressed themselves was to say that the 'day of the Lord' had come, 'the great and manifest day',[15] which would bring to an end this present world and inaugurate the new age. The sign of this was the outpouring of the Spirit. The Spirit (*ruah*) in Hebrew tradition is the power of God, the power by which he creates the world and sustains it by his immanent presence. 'The Spirit of the Lord has filled the world.'[16] But at the end of time this spirit was to be poured out on all flesh. The sign of the 'last days' would be that man and creation would be transformed by this power of the Spirit, and that was what was believed to have taken place at Pentecost. The passage from this world to the other world had taken place by the transformation of human consciousness through the power of the Spirit. But this transformation and outpouring of the Spirit was seen to have come through the death of Jesus on the Cross. He had gone through death and had been taken up into the life of God. This was expressed by saying that 'this Jesus whom you crucified God has made Lord and Christ'.[17] By saying that Jesus was the Christ, that is, the Messiah, it was signified that in him the expectations of Israel had been fulfilled and the Kingdom promised to David had now come. By saying that Jesus was the 'Lord' it was signified that Jesus had been placed on an equality with God. 'The Lord' was the name for God in the Old Testament, and Jesus's relation to God was expressed in mythological terms as being seated 'at the right hand of God'.

This was the language in which the Christian experience was first expressed. Then other terms were added. Jesus was the 'Son of God', of whom it was said in the Psalm: 'You are my Son, this day have I begotten you'.[18] He was also the

Son of Man, of whom it was said in the book of Daniel: 'I saw one like to a son of man coming on the clouds of heaven, and there was given to him dominion and glory and a kingdom, that all the peoples, nations and languages should serve him.'[19] Further he was seen as the great Prophet who was to come into the world, who should speak in the name of God.[20] Again he was seen as the great High Priest, the Mediator between God and Man.[21] Finally he came to be seen as the Word of God,[22] the expression of the mind of God, the self-revelation of the absolute. Thus the Christian myth was gradually built up, a revelation of the supreme Truth in symbolic language, springing from the experience of the disciples of Christ after Pentecost, when in the light of the Spirit, through their transformed consciousness, they realized who and what this Jesus was whom they had known. This remains the essential Christian experience – the experience of absolute reality, absolute truth and absolute bliss – in Hindu terms *Saccidananda* – in and through the person of Jesus of Nazareth and the event of his death on the Cross.

This was interpreted in terms of 'resurrection'. Stories grew up that his tomb had been found empty, that he had appeared to his disciples after his death. What are we to make of those stories? It would not do to take them simply as historical facts. They are records of an experience, a psychological and a mystical experience. The essence of this experience was that it was an experience of God. God, the absolute reality, had been encountered in Jesus. Jesus was the Lord, the Son of God, the Word of God, in whom the ultimate meaning and purpose of human existence had been revealed. Nevertheless, the empty tomb and the appearances after death have their place. We have seen that in the view of the ancient world, and increasingly of the modern world, the universe has three levels of reality: the physical, the psychological and the spiritual. These three 'worlds' form an interdependent whole. The physical world cannot be separated from the world of Spirit, of ultimate reality. The resurrection of Jesus is a sign of this integral reality. His physical body did not disintegrate, but was reunited with his soul, his psyche. Soul and body did not 'disappear' but were transfigured by the indwelling Spirit. This reveals the ultimate destiny of man. Soul and body are not destined to 'disappear' in the final state of being. The physical body, and with it the whole organic universe – the field of energies – to which it belongs are destined to be totally transformed by consciousness, not left in their present divided state. Human consciousness in turn is destined to be transformed by the divine consciousness, no longer subject to space and time but integrated in the eternal and infinite consciousness of ultimate reality. The Resurrection of Jesus is a sign of this transformation. His body was not found in the tomb. He appeared to his disciples after his death in his own form, revealing the continuity of his human consciousness. But his body was no longer subject to the laws of matter and his human consciousness had now been transformed by the divine consciousness.

This principle enables us to understand the Virgin Birth and the miracles of Jesus, which have caused so much difficulty to those brought up in the scientific tradition of the West. As long as matter is imagined to be something separate from mind, an 'extended substance' with its own necessary laws, then miracles have either to be dismissed altogether or explained as the arbitrary acts of a transcendent God. But once it is understood that mind and matter are interdependent, that the universe is a psychosomatic unity, then there is no serious problem. The evolution of the world is seen as the progressive penetration of matter by consciousness, latent in the inorganic world, beginning to become manifest in plant and animal, and fully manifest in man. Further human evolution is then seen as the growth in conscious awareness and consequently conscious control. From the Shamans of the American Indian tradition, through the various forms of magic in Egypt and China, and elsewhere to the *siddhis* of the Hindu tradition, there is continuous evidence of the existence of these 'supernatural' powers, that is, the conscious control over the body and the natural world by human beings. In Jesus, as in many of the saints of all religions, these powers were clearly manifested – power over disease and 'evil spirits', that is daemonic powers, power over nature as in the multiplication of bread and conversion of water into wine. Such powers are by no means unusual and are not necessarily of the spiritual order. They are rather 'psychic' powers, powers of the human psyche either innate or developed by various techniques. In Jesus, of course, as in other religious leaders, these powers came under the control of the Spirit and were manifestations of the divine Spirit in man.

In this way it is not difficult to understand the Virgin Birth. Virgin Birth is a mythological conception of great antiquity and would seem to indicate a basic urge in human nature to transcend the present level of sexuality. Sexuality is part of our inheritance from the animals, and in human nature there is an instinctive urge to transcend the physical level of sexuality and realize it at a deeper psychological and spiritual level. Ultimately, sexuality is the energy of love in human nature, and this can never be satisfied at either the physical or the psychological level, but always seeks fulfilment in the depth of the spirit, where it encounters the source of love. In a sense the whole creation can be seen as a 'marriage' between matter and mind, nature and spirit,

Prakriti and *Purusha*, in Hindu terms, and every human marriage is a reflection of this cosmic union. In the biblical tradition the people of Israel were seen as the 'bride' of Yahweh and the climax of Israel's history was to be the marriage of Israel, the people of God, with its God. In the famous prophecy of Isaiah, where it is said 'the virgin shall be with child',[23] it has been suggested that the young woman, the *alma*, who was to be the mother of the Messiah, refers to the Virgin of Israel, the representative of woman before God, in whom the fulfilment of human destiny is achieved. In her the evolution of body and soul was to reach a point at which the transformation of sexuality by the power of the indwelling Spirit could take place, and the marriage of God and man could be consummated. Such a transformation of sexuality is the destiny of all men and women, when the Spirit finally takes possession of human nature and transfigures it. The Virgin Birth of Jesus is thus the historic sign of this universal cosmic mystery.

We can speak therefore of the Virgin Birth of Jesus and the Resurrection as mythical history. They are myths or revelations of the ultimate mystery of existence, which are grounded in a unique historic tradition and centred on a unique historic event. How, then, are we to understand the 'divinity' of Jesus? That Jesus was a man is basic to a Christian understanding of life. He stands within a clearly defined, historic tradition, and we know as much about him as we do, for instance, about Socrates. Yet at the same time his disciples came to recognize him as 'Son of God'. The language is, of course, mythological, but it expresses clearly the idea of equality with God. But for the Jews this presented a serious problem. They were convinced that there was but one God. The religion of Israel was founded on this faith. Was it then possible to speak of Jesus as God? The New Testament as a whole refuses to do so. It speaks of him as 'son' of God, 'image' of God, 'word' of God, but all these words imply in some way equality with God. The answer to this problem was eventually found in the concept of relationship. Son, image, word, all imply relationship, and, when the disciples of Jesus came to reflect on this question, they saw that to say that Jesus was son of God was to imply that he stood in a unique relation to God, as a son to a father. But there is clearly a sense in which all men are sons of God. Man is created in the 'image and likeness' of God; he is created to 'share in the divine nature'. What was revealed in Jesus was the destiny of all men. He is the exemplar in whom the destiny of man was seen to be fulfilled. From the beginning of creation Man had been called to fulfil this destiny, to become a Son of God, but in all men there is some sin, some defect, which prevents this fulfilment. In Jesus a man was found, fully a man and centred in history, a Jew of Palestine in the first century, in whom there was no defect; body and soul were so perfectly under the control of the indwelling Spirit, that they became its instruments, responding totally to its impulse. In him the Spirit was not limited by a defective body and soul, but could act freely, expressing the will of his Father at every moment, surrendering to his will to the point of death on the Cross, and in the Resurrection, taking complete possession of body and soul, so as to transfigure them by its power.

Jesus therefore was a man, in whom body and soul were pure instruments of the indwelling Spirit. In him the destiny of man has been fulfilled. But this inevitably has an effect on the whole cosmos. The universe is a psychosomatic unity, a space-time continuum, in which each part depends on every other part as an integrated whole. Whereas in the universe, as we know it, there is conflict at every level, and body and soul are in conflict with one another, in Jesus this conflict has been overcome, body and soul have been restored to unity with the Spirit, and a power of unification has been released in the world. In this sense we can say that the death of Jesus, the free surrender of his life on the Cross to his Father, was a cosmic event. Every event in time and history affects in some measure the whole creation, since all the elements of the world are interdependent. But certain events, the emergence of life on this planet, the awakening of consciousness in man, mark critical stages in the evolution of the world. The death of Jesus was an event of this kind. It marked the point of transcendence of the human consciousness to the divine; the point where the human being was totally surrendered, body and soul, to the divine being. In this sense the death of Jesus can be called a 'redemptive sacrifice'; it is an offering of human nature to the divine which 'redeems', that is restores human nature to its unity with the divine nature. The Resurrection, the transcendence of death by Jesus in body and in soul, is the historic sign of this cosmic redemption, the sign that not only the soul, the psychic being, but also the body, the physical creation, has been liberated from its present bondage and has become a 'new creation'.

But what does this signify in regard to the psychology of Jesus? As a man Jesus had a physical organism with all the effects of heredity, as a Jew, from his mother, and his body was subject to all the normal effects of nature. He had to grow and mature, as St Luke's Gospel says: 'the boy Jesus increased in wisdom and in stature'.[24] He was subject to pain and stress, even to the point of sweating blood.[25] His soul also, his psychic organism, was that of a Jew of his time and place. He had to learn his mother tongue, to read and meditate the sacred scriptures in order to discover his vocation. There is every reason to think that it was only gradually that he realized his calling as Messiah and the fact that it would lead to death on a cross. At the moment of death he experienced in his soul the tragic sense of separation from God, when he cried out: 'My God, my God, why hast thou forsaken me?'[26]

But behind all this human experience of body and of soul, there was also the intuitive knowledge of the spirit. In the depths of his being, like every human being, he was present to himself, aware of himself, in relation to the eternal ground of his being. In most people this intuitive awareness is inchoate or imperfect, but in the great prophet and mystic, in the seer like Gautama Buddha or the seers of the Upanishads, this intuitive knowledge of the ground of being becomes a pure intuition, a total awareness. Such according to the tradition of St John's Gospel (which in its origin is now considered to be as old as that of the other gospels)[27] was the nature of the knowledge of Jesus. He knew himself in the depth of his spirit as one with the eternal ground of his being, which he spoke of as the Father. He knew himself as standing in a relationship of total dependence on the Father and of total surrender to him. He knew himself as expressing the mind and will of the Father, and of accomplishing his purpose for the world. It is this that is signified by his calling himself Son. At the same time he knew himself to be 'anointed'[28] with the Holy Spirit, the spirit that is present in the whole creation and in all humanity, but in him was present as a 'spirit of holiness', the presence of God in his own essential being (which is what holiness signifies) communicating himself in love. It is from this experience of Jesus in the Spirit, as it was revealed by his intuitive insight to the apostle John, that the doctrine of the Trinity was evolved.

The doctrine of the Trinity was developed from St John's Gospel by the Greek fathers, using the language of Greek conceptual thought, in terms of essence and nature and person and relation, and this has become the normal form of the doctrine in Christian tradition. But it is possible that the same experience could be interpreted in other terms, drawn from a different tradition. In Hinduism the experience of God was expressed, as we have seen, in terms of *Brahman, Atman,* and *Purusha.* Would it not be possible to interpret the experience of Jesus in the light of the Hindu understanding of ultimate reality? We could then speak of God as *Saccidananda* – Being, Knowledge, Bliss – and see in the Father, *sat,* Being, the absolute eternal 'I am', the ground of Being, the source of all. We could then speak of the Son, as the *cit,* the knowledge of the Father, the Self-consciousness of eternal Being, the presence to itself in pure consciousness of the infinite One; Being reflecting on itself, knowing itself, expressing itself in an eternal Word. We could then speak of the Father as *niriguna Brahman,* Brahman 'without attributes', the infinite abyss of being beyond word and thought. The Son would then be *Saguna Brahman,* Brahman 'with attributes', as Creator, Lord, Saviour, the Self-manifestation of the unmanifest God, the personal aspect of the Godhead, the *Purusha.* He is that 'supreme person', (*Purushottaman*) of the Bhagavad Gita, the 'unborn, beginningless, great Lord of the world',[29] the 'supreme Brahman, the supreme abode, the supreme purity, the eternal divine Person (*purusha*), the primal God (*adideva*), the unborn, the omnipresent (*vibhum*)'.[30]

Finally, we could speak of the spirit as the *Ananda,* the Bliss or Joy of the Godhead, the outpouring of the super-abundant being and consciousness of the eternal, the Love which unites Father and Son in the non-dual Being of the Spirit. This spirit is also the *Atman,* the Breath (*pneuma*) of God, which is in all creation and gives life to every living thing, which in man becomes conscious and grows with the growth of conscious-ness, until it becomes pure, intuitive wisdom. The *Atman* is the spirit of God in man, when the human spirit becomes wholly pervaded by the divine spirit and attains to pure consciousness. It is conscious Bliss, consciousness filled with joy, with the delight of Being. This was the spirit which filled the soul of Jesus and gave him perfect consciousness of his relationship as Son to the eternal ground of being in the Godhead.

Hindu experience can also help to bring out another aspect of the godhead, the concept of God as Mother. The Hebrew tradition was patriarchal and Christianity has preserved only a masculine concept of God. The Father and the Son are masculine in their very names, and even the Spirit, which is neuter in Greek, has been given a masculine character. But the Hebrew tradition also preserves a word for the spirit (*ruah*) which is feminine, and in the Syrian Church this feminine gender was preserved, so that they could speak of the Holy Spirit as Mother. There is also in the Old Testament the beautiful figure of Wisdom (*hocmah*) which is also feminine. In this we can find a truly feminine aspect of God, when it is said: 'She is a breath of the power of God and a pure emanation of the glory of the almighty' and again; 'she is a reflection of eternal light and a spotless mirror of the working of God . . . though she is but one, she can do all things, and remaining in herself, she renews all things'.[31] In this sense we can speak of God as Mother no less than Father, and even the Son, as the Word of God, can be called the Daughter of God, as when it is said: 'I came forth from the mouth of the Most High.'[32]

But it is in the Holy Spirit that the feminine aspect of the godhead can be most clearly seen. She is the *Sakti*, the power, immanent in all creation, the *receptive* power of the Godhead. The world comes forth from the Father, the eternal Ground of Being, in his Word, the Cosmic Person (*purusha*). In him the ideas or archetypes of all created beings are hidden; he is the exemplar of all creation. But it is the Spirit who conceives these 'ideas' in her maternal womb and brings them forth in creation. She is the Great Mother (the *Devi*) who nourishes the seeds of all beings and makes them grow. Still more, she is the mothering Spirit in man, who receives the Word, the Wisdom of God, in her heart, of whom in the Christian tradition Mary is the figure, receiving the Word of God in her heart and bringing him forth in his earthly manifestation. Even in the bosom of the Godhead itself, the Spirit is the eternal feminine, who on the one hand receives the Word of God coming from the Father, and on the other is the Bride of the Son, through whom the creation is conceived and brought into being.

III

THE MYTH OF THE CHURCH

In Christian tradition the figure of the Mother is found in the Church. In an early Christian writing, *The Shepherd of Hermas*, the Church appears in the form of an old woman. When it is asked why she appears as an old woman, the answer is given: 'Because she was created first of all. On this account is she old, and for her sake was the world made.'[33] It is necessary to see the Church in this cosmic aspect. The Church as a historical institution has a very recent origin and occupies a very small part of the world. But the Church in herself is the eternal Mother; she is the created aspect of the uncreated Spirit. 'For her sake was the world made.' The world in a real sense is the 'becoming' of God. He, who is infinite, unchanging being in himself, reveals himself, expresses himself, in the finite, changing nature of the world.

The eternal Word, in whom the 'archetypes' of all created beings exist eternally, manifests himself in time. The whole creation, from the smallest atom to the furthest star, is a manifestation in space and time, in multiplicity and change, of that unchanging One. The Spirit, immanent in nature from the beginning, receives these 'seeds of the word' into her womb and brings them forth in creation. From the first beginning of matter, through all the stages of evolution, of organic growth and consciousness, the Spirit is structuring these forms, moulding them by her inherent power.

In man this Spirit is at work organizing the chemicals which make up his body, building up the cells, developing the nerves and the muscles and the glands, structuring the organs of touch and taste, of smell and sight and hearing, finally bringing all this complex organism, through the elaborate structure of the brain, into consciousness. With consciousness, Nature, the Mother, awakens to a new mode of being, and begins to discover, to become conscious of, her meaning and destiny. Over millions of years the Spirit is working through Nature, responding to the action of the Word, the Cosmic Person, the *Purusha*, who unites himself with his bride, his *Sakti*, to bring forth this world. As consciousness grows in man, Nature becomes conscious of the immanent power within her and the Church is born.

The Church is Man become conscious of his destiny as a son of God. In the biblical perspective Adam is Man, created in the image and likeness of God, and called to be a son of God. When Adam sins, he fails in his calling; he fails to respond to the Spirit, and falls back on his limited time-bound nature. The upward movement of evolution from matter through life and consciousness to eternal life in the Spirit is checked. But at the same time the mystery of redemption begins. A new power of the Spirit, the *Sakti*, enters the creation and begins to draw man back into the life of the Spirit. This is the beginning of the Church, humanity drawn out of sin by the power of the Spirit and responding to the Word of God. In this sense, the Church is present in humanity from the beginning of history. Wherever man wakes to consciousness and knows himself in his basic intuitive consciousness as open to the transcendent mystery of existence, the power of the Spirit is in him, drawing him to eternal life. The presence of the Spirit in this sense can be traced in all the religions of mankind. Everywhere, in ritual and sacrifice, in doctrine and sacrament, in prayer and worship, there is a presence of the Spirit drawing man to God, a response to the Word of God seeking to unite mankind with himself: in other words, a presence of the Church. We need to recover this understanding of the Universal Church, the Church which was 'created first of all . . . for whose sake was the world made'.

It is not only the whole of humanity but the whole creation which constitutes the body of the Church. Matter was created from the beginning with an innate tendency towards life and consciousness. Human consciousness was created from the beginning with an innate tendency towards the final and perfect consciousness of the Spirit. The same Spirit was present in matter, in life and in man, from the beginning drawing him towards itself. In Jesus this movement of matter and consciousness towards the life of the Spirit reached its culmination. In him the divine consciousness took possession of human consciousness, and both body and soul, matter and consciousness, were transformed. In him the marriage of God and Man, of Nature and Spirit, of *Purusha* and *Prakriti*, was consummated.

But this consummation of the union of God with man in Jesus necessarily affects the whole creation. This was the consummation for which the whole creation had been 'groaning in travail', as St Paul says, from the beginning. The whole creation is an organic unity just as Man himself is an organic unity. At the Resurrection Jesus becomes the 'head' of this Cosmic whole, and the whole creation becomes his Body, and this Body of creation, redeemed from the forces of sin and division, is what constitutes the Church. 'He has put all things under his feet,' says St Paul, 'and made him the head over all things for the Church, which is his body, the fullness of him who fills all in all.'[34] The Church is the Pleroma, the fullness, the consummation of all things, the term of the whole evolutionary process. The divine *Purusha* has taken possession of *Prakriti*, Nature, and filled her with his presence. In other words Nature has been wholly penetrated with consciousness, and Man and Nature have become one with the eternal Spirit. The Resurrection thus reveals the plan of the whole creation. What was accomplished in Jesus through his sacrificial death and his rebirth to eternal life, is what is destined to happen in all men and in all creation. We are all members of this fallen and redeemed humanity, each of us bearing in himself the marks of the Fall, of sin and suffering and death, and each of us is called to pass beyond sin and suffering and death into the new life of the Resurrection. 'The first Adam,' it is said, 'was a living soul, the second Adam became a life-giving spirit.'[35] The 'Word became flesh',[36] the divine Spirit entered into the depths of matter, of life and of consciousness, into the midst of human sin and suffering, and raised up this fallen world to new life and new consciousness in himself. Thus the Church is present in all creation and in all humanity; it is the 'becoming' of God, the manifestation of the infinite, eternal Being in the course of time and change and history, not simply as a static presence, but as a dynamic power, changing the course of history and transforming the world.

For while the Church has this cosmic dimension, this universal character, it is also a historical institution. This is in accordance with the biblical tradition, which while it looks towards the final consummation of creation and man, at the same time sees this great Myth rooted in historic time and place. Jesus, who is the cosmic Lord and Universal Saviour, is also the man who was 'crucified under Pontius Pilate'. So also the Church, which is the consummation of the world and of history, has its beginning in time. While the Bible sees the plan of God extending to all humanity, from the first to the second Adam, it also sees it working out in the history of a particular people and coming to a head at a particular time. Jesus comes announcing the coming of the kingdom of God: 'The Kingdom of God is at hand,'[37] and he prepares a group of disciples to whom this 'mystery' of the kingdom of God is entrusted. They are to be the nucleus of the 'people of God', the new humanity, which comes to birth through his death and resurrection. At Pentecost this new humanity comes into being; the Spirit descends and transforms the disciples by his power and presence. A new age begins in which this power of the Spirit is to spread through the world and humanity is to be gathered into the kingdom of God. Such is the mission of the earthly Church, to be the witness, or rather the embodiment, of the power of the Spirit, acting as a leaven in creation and bringing it to fulfilment in the kingdom of God.

But once the Church enters into the world, it becomes subject to all the vicissitudes of time and change. This is the hazard which faces every religion. The spirit which inspired the religion, which is the presence of God himself, becomes overshadowed by human sins and infirmity. When we look at the Christian Churches today and recall their history, it often seems more like a record of human sin than of divine grace. If we look deep enough, we shall see that the Spirit of God is always present, changing people's lives, moving them to love and service, often effecting radical changes in society, inspiring people with ideals of sacrifice, with visions of truth, with the fire of mystical experience. But the other side, not only of sin, but of human limitations, of cultural blindness, above all of narrowness of mind and fanaticism, is only too evident. If the Myth of the Church is to be revived today, it must find new forms of expression. Its universal meaning has to be discovered, its relationship to all the religious traditions of mankind, its relevance to the world in which we live. Such a rebirth of the Myth of the Church is already taking place, but it still has a long way to go. Above all, we have to discover the source of those deformations which have afflicted all the Churches and have led to their present state.

We have first of all to consider the cultural limitations of Christianity. It was the product of a Semitic culture which had a very narrow horizon. Israel grew up in the small world of the Middle East, bounded by Egypt on one side and Babylonia on the other. Influences from Persia and from Greece later came to enrich it, but its vision, though profound, remained very limited. It had no knowledge of the cultures of India or China or the rest of the world, and imagined that all those who were outside Israel were without knowledge of God, just as the Greeks imagined that all who were not Greeks were 'barbarians'. Also, its vision was temporally very limited, so that it did not extend beyond the year 5000 BC and imagined that it was living in the 'last age' of the world.

It was from this milieu and with these limitations that the Christian Church came out into the Graeco-Roman world. The Greeks brought with them their genius for philosophy, and the Romans their genius for law, and the theology and organization of the Church were built up by these means. This certainly gave the Church a profound theology and a powerful organization but it also brought grave limitations. Greek philosophy was essentially a rational philosophy, and though Plato brought to it the insights of intuitive wisdom, its influence was more and more felt in the development of logical rational thought and scientific system which are characteristic of Western man. The Church thus became dominated by that system of rational thought, which is the cause of the imbalance of the Western world, though the imaginative insight and intuitive wisdom of the biblical tradition was never wholly lost. The result of this was that the Church became obsessed with the need to construct logical formulas and rational systems by which to express its faith. When these formulas or 'dogmas' came to be reinforced by the legal system of Rome, the Inquisition came into being, and the attempt was made to impose this doctrinal system by force. The Reformation was a revolt against this rational legal system and sought to set the Church free by a return to the Bible, but again the Western mind introduced its logical formulas and legal systems and each church set itself up as alone professing the true faith. The result is that the Church today consists of innumerable sects, each claiming to represent the true faith and denouncing the others as 'heretical'. The ecumenical movement has come to seek to overcome these divisions and to return to the unity of the Church, but unless it abandons the search for doctrinal formulas and legal systems, and recovers the intuitive wisdom of the Bible and of ancient man, there is little hope of success.

It is here that the encounter with Eastern thought, with its intuitive basis, is crucial. Christianity cannot grow as a religion today, unless it abandons its Western culture with its rational masculine bias and learns again the feminine intuitive understanding of the East. The suppression of women in the Church is but one of the many signs of this masculine domination. This does not mean, of course, that the real values of science and reason, of logical and systematic thought have to be abandoned. Reason has to be 'married' to intuition; it has to learn to surrender itself to the deeper intuitions of the Spirit. These intuitions come, as we have seen, from the presence of the Spirit in the depths of the soul. They are an expression of a growing self-awareness, of an integral knowledge not of the mind or reason alone, but of the whole man, body, soul and spirit. Faith itself is a function not of the rational but of the intuitive mind. It does not consist, as Western man has often thought, in an assent to logical propositions, but in a grasp of the 'mystery' of truth as a whole. The intuitive mind, it will be remembered, does not analyse but grasps the whole, or rather opens itself to the whole, allows it to take possession. So faith opens itself to the mystery of God, to the unfathomable truth and allows it to take possession of the soul. So for a Christian faith is an openness to the mystery of God in Christ mediated through the myth of Christ. The myth appeals to the imagination, to the heart, and transforms the person. Later, reason may come to distinguish different aspects of the myth and relate them to one another, but always a return must be made to the 'mystery', to the reality, which both myth and reason seek to express.

The reunion of the Christian churches can only come, therefore, through a rediscovery of the 'mystery of Christ' in all its dimensions, and this means that it must be related to the whole history of humanity and of the creation. This will only come when we have learned to discover the presence of this mystery, that is, of the Church, in all the religions of mankind. Every genuine religion bears witness to some aspect of the divine mystery, embodied in its myths and rituals, its customs and traditions, its prayer and mystical experience, and each has something to give to the universal Church. The narrow-mindedness which has divided the Christian churches from one another, has also divided the Christian religion from other religions. Today we have to open ourselves to the truth in all religions. Each religion must learn to discern its essential truth and to reject its cultural and historical limitations. This may be a painful experience, a rejection of innumerable elements in religion which have grown up with the cultural and historical development of a religion and have often been identified with the religion itself. Yet this seems to be the only path open to humanity today. What stands in the way is the dominant mentality of the Western world. This is the hour of trial for Western man. Will he continue to build up his scientific world with nuclear power leading to the devastation of the earth, or will he learn to repent, to turn back, to rediscover the source of life, the wisdom of Mother Earth, which is also the wisdom of the East?

The Church also has to learn the secret of this intuitive wisdom. Though the Mystery of Christ is always present in the Church, and is the secret presence by which she lives, yet the doctrinal and sacramental structures of the Church are all the product of the Western mind, whether it is Roman Catholicism or Greek Orthodoxy, or Anglicanism, Lutheranism or Calvinism, or the various Protestant Churches in Britain and America. All alike are developments of the Mystery of Christ produced by the Western mind. Neither papacy nor episcopacy or any other system of church government is found in the New Testament. They are the work of the Greek and Roman genius, building on the foundation of the New Testament. Jesus himself gave no system of government to the Church. He founded it on twelve disciples to represent the new Israel, the new people of God, and according to the earliest tradition, gave Peter, as the Rock (*Cephas*), a position of leadership in it; he also gave it by all accounts the sacramental rites of Baptism and the Eucharist. But beyond this he left everything to the guidance of the Holy Spirit, who was to lead his disciples into all truth. All that has been erected on this foundation, all doctrinal and sacramental and legal systems, are the work of the Western mind, guided no doubt by the Holy Spirit in varying degrees, but all alike conditioned by historical circumstances.

The fact that Rome became the centre of Christendom is an accident of history and the Bishop of Rome only acquired his present position after many centuries. One may hold that this development was providential, but there is no reason to believe that the present structure of the papacy is permanent, or that the Church may not acquire a new structure in the context of future history.

In the same way, episcopacy as a system of government was only gradually established and there is no reason to hold that the present structure, whether in its Roman or Greek or Anglican or Lutheran form, should always remain. All church structures are subject to the law of historical growth.

In the same way the doctrinal structures, built up by the Western mind on the foundations of the faith of the apostles, are all historically conditioned and bear the mark of the limitations of the Western mind. It is certain that the people of Asia will never accept Christianity in its present form. Five centuries and more of missionary activity have shown the futility of the attempt. Christianity remains for the people of the East a foreign religion, moulded by the Western mind.

We have to go beyond all these historical structures and

recover the original Myth of Christianity, the living truth which was revealed in the New Testament. But this cannot be done by the Western mind alone. We have to open ourselves to the revelation of the divine mystery, which took place in Asia, in Hinduism and Buddhism, in Taoism, Confucianism and Shintoism. Nor can we neglect the intuitive wisdom of more primitive people, the Australian Aborigines, the Polynesian Islanders, the African Bushmen, the American Indians, the Eskimoes. All over the world the supreme Spirit has left signs of his presence. The Christian mystery is the mystery of God's presence in Man, and we cannot neglect any sign of that presence. Even the atheist and the agnostic can bear witness to this mystery. Atheism and agnosticism signify the rejection of certain images and concepts of God or of Truth, which are historically conditioned and therefore inadequate. Atheism is a challenge to religion to purify its images and concepts and come nearer to the truth of the divine mystery.

We have always to bear in mind that the divine Mystery, the ultimate Truth, always lies beyond our conception. The great Myths of the world reveal different aspects of this mystery according to the imaginative insight of the different peoples of the world. In Jesus the Myth took a particular historical form which is recorded in the New Testament and preserved in the Church. But the Myth is capable of ever new understanding as the human mind reflects upon it. It has been given a particular rational and legal structure by the Western mind, but the Eastern mind and the primitive intuitive mind throughout the world is capable of discovering new depths of meaning in it, and the modern Western mind, freed from the shackles of a mechanistic model of the universe, is capable of rediscovering the meaning of the Myth. The building of the Church as the manifestation in history of the presence of

God in man, is therefore the work of all mankind. The Hindu, the Buddhist, the Muslim, the humanist, the philosopher, the scientist, have all something to give and something to receive. The Christian, to whatever church he may belong, cannot claim to have the monopoly of the Truth. We are all pilgrims in search of truth, of reality, of final fulfilment. But we have to recognize that this Truth will always remain beyond our understanding. No science or philosophy or theology can ever encompass the Truth. No poetry or art or human institution can ever embody it. The great Myths are only reflections in the human imagination of that transcendent Mystery. Even the Myth of Christ belongs still to the world of signs, and we have to go beyond the Myth to the Mystery itself, beyond word and thought, beyond life and death. For the ultimate Mystery can only be known through the passage of death. 'You have died,' wrote St Paul, 'and your life is hidden with Christ in God; when Christ who is our life appears, you also will appear with him in glory.'[38]

Jesus left his disciples with the expectation that he would appear again and bring this world to an end. This is the condition under which we all live. At no time in history has the world been nearer to destruction than it is at the present moment. There are forces present in the world which are capable of destroying all life on this planet and those who control these forces are themselves beyond control. It may be that the Western world will change, or at least a sufficient number will be there to initiate a change, to undergo a *metanoia*, a change of heart, and set the world on another course, bringing about the marriage of East and West. But there can be no finality even in this. Our destiny is not in this world, and we have to be prepared to go beyond death. We have to die to this world and everything in it, that is, everything that changes and passes in this world, to find the reality which does not change or pass. Above all, we have to go beyond words and images and concepts. No imaginative vision or conceptual framework is adequate to the great reality. When Christ will appear in glory, it will not be in any earthly form or in any manner we can conceive. 'For now we see in a mirror dimly, but then face to face;'[39] and we shall only 'appear in glory', when we have died to ourselves and become a 'new creation'.[40] Then alone shall we encounter the fullness of truth and reality which is also the fullness of wisdom and knowledge and the fullness of bliss and love. Then only will the final marriage take place, of East and West, of man and woman, of matter and mind, of time and eternity.

Notes

I

The Discovery of India

1 *The Golden String* was published by the Harvill Press in 1954 and by Collins in Fontana Books in 1964. It was reprinted in 1979.

2 Recently Dr Panikkar published *The Vedic Experience*, a translation of the principal texts of the Vedas with notes and commentary, showing the relevance of the Vedas for modern man. It was published by Darton, Longman and Todd in 1978.

3 A fuller account of this foundation will be found in *Christian Ashram*, published by Darton, Longman and Todd in 1966.

4 Father Monchanin's life and some of his writings were published under the title *The Quest of the Absolute*, edited by J. G. Weber, in 1977 by Cistercian Publications in the US, and by Mowbray, Oxford. Father Le Saux's books, written under the name of Abhishiktananda, are published by the ISPCK in Delhi, and his book on prayer has also been published by the SPCK in London.

5 Svetasvatara Upanishad, 2:17.

6 cf. *The Tao of Physics* by Fritjof Capra in Fontana Books, 1976. This is the most remarkable example of a Western scientist discovering the values of Eastern thought. That this is not the view only of an individual scientist but of scientific orthodoxy is shown by Bernard Despagnat in *Conceptual Foundations of Quantum Mechanics* (Benjamin Inc., 1976).

7 cf. *The Tao of Physics*, page 142.

8 Quoted in *The Tao of Physics*, page 144.

9 Wisdom of Solomon, 1:7.

10 John 1:13.

11 cf. 2 Corinthians 5:17 and Galatians 6:15.

12 John 17:23.

13 Acts 4:32.

14 Acts 3:21.

15 2 Peter 3:8.

16 1 Corinthians 12:3.

17 Ephesians 4:5–6.

18 Acts 1:3.

19 John 16:7.

20 John 12:24.

21 In the Epilogue to *The Golden String*.

22 Chandogya Upanishad 8:1:3.

23 John 1:4. According to one reading: 'All that was made was life in him.'

24 Galatians 5:22: 'The fruits of the Spirit are these, love, peace, joy . . .'

II

The Vedic Revelation

I

THE VEDIC MYTH

1 Giambattista Vico (1688–1744), author of *Scienza Nuova* (*The New Science*), seems to have been the first European philosopher to realize the significance of myth and poetry.

2 The great authority on Myth today is Mircea Eliade. See especially: *Myths, Dreams and Mysteries* (English translation published by the Harvill Press, 1960). *Images and Symbols* (English translation by Harvill Press, 1961). *Myth and Reality in World Perspectives* (Allen and Unwin, 1963).

3 *Poetic Diction* by Owen Barfield. Second edition, Faber & Faber, 1952.

4 *On the Vedas* by Sri Aurobindo (published by Aurobindo Ashram, Pondicherry).

Notes

5 Quoted in *The Tao of Physics*, page 144.

6 Bernard D'Espagnat in *Conceptual Foundations of Quantum Mechanics*.

7 'An appearance of being, without origin, inexpressible in terms of being or of not-being.' Sankara's commentary on the Brahma Sutras.

8 The most profound study of the Vedic Myth that I know and of the significance of the Vedic Revelation is that of Jeanine Miller: *The Vedas* (Rider, 1974).

9 cf. Ephesians 1:21; 3:10; 6:12 and Colossians 1:16; 2:15, 18, 20. For St Paul these 'powers' are both good and evil, like the *devas* and *asuras* of the Vedic tradition.

10 cf. 1 Thessalonians 5:23 and the contrast between the '*anthropos psychikos*', the 'psychic man', and the '*anthropos pneumatikos*', the 'spiritual man', in 1 Corinthians 2:14.

11 Romans 8:16.

II

THE REVELATION OF THE UPANISHADS

12 *On the Vedas*, ch. 5, 'The Philological Method of the Vedas.'

13 Brihadaranyaka Upanishad 1:4.11.

14 Brihadaranyaka Upanishad 2:5.

15 Chandogya Upanishad 4:14:1.

16 Brihadaranyaka Upanishad 2:3:6.

17 Chandogya Upanishad 8:7–12.

18 cf. Rig Veda 1:164.46: 'The one being (*ekam sat*) the wise call by many names.'

19 Katha Upanishad 2:23.

20 Romans 6:3.

21 Katha Upanishad 2:9.

22 Katha Upanishad 2:12.

23 Rig Veda 10:90.

24 Chandogya Upanishad 8:3.

25 Katha Upanishad 3:10–11.

26 Brihadaranyaka Upanishad 4:3:7.

27 Katha Upanishad 3:13.

28 Brihadaranyaka Upanishad 3:8:11.

29 Katha Upanishad 2:23.

30 Katha Upanishad 3:1.
31 Svetasvatara Upanishad 4:6–7.
32 1 Corinthians 2:12.
33 1 Corinthians 2:14–15.
34 Svetasvatara Upanishad 2:14–15.

III

THE REVELATION OF THE PERSONAL GOD

35 Brihadaranyaka Upanishad 4:4:15.
36 Isa Upanishad 1.
37 Svetasvatara Upanishad 1:7–9.
38 Non-duality, qualified non-duality, and duality.
39 Svetasvatara Upanishad 3:7.
40 Svetasvatara Upanishad 3:9:11.
41 cf. *The Love of God in Saiva Siddhanta* by M. Dhavamony. (OUP, 1971), Part 3.1b.
42 Svetasvatara Upanishad 3:19.
43 Svetasvatara Upanishad 3:12.
44 Svetasvatara Upanishad 3:13.
45 Svetasvatara Upanishad 6:7.
46 Svetasvatara Upanishad 5:11–12.
47 *Summa Theologica* 1:8:3.
48 Acts of the Apostles 17:28.
49 *Summa Theologica* 1:15:1 ad 3.
50 Bhagavad Gita 9:4–5.
51 Bhagavad Gita 5:20.
52 Bhagavad Gita 5:21.
53 Bhagavad Gita 5:29. cf. also 6:29. 'He sees the Self abiding in all beings and all beings in the Self', followed by 6:30: 'He sees me in all things and all things in me.'
54 Bhagavad Gita 15:16–17.

Notes

IV

THE DOCTRINE OF NON-DUALITY

55 Romans 1:20.
56 Brihadaranyaka Upanishad 3:7:23.
57 Brihadaranyaka Upanishad 2:4:13.
58 Commentary on the Taittiriya Upanishad 2:1.
59 *Unus Christus amans seipsum.*
60 This theory has been developed at length by Karl Rahner. See especially *Foundations of Christian Faith*, 1, 3, 'Man as Transcendent Being' (Darton, Longman and Todd, 1978).
61 Katha Upanishad 2:23.
62 cf. also Taittiriya Upanishad 3:2–6 on the five 'sheaths' (*Kosas*) of consciousness.

V

THE SUPREME SECRET

63 Bhagavad Gita 7:17 and 18:65.
64 Taittiriya Upanishad 2:2.
65 John 14:10.
66 John 17:21.
67 Romans 8:16.
68 Plotinus, *Enneads* 5:8:4.
69 2 Corinthians 3:18.

III

The Judaic Revelation

I

THE MYTHOLOGY OF THE OLD TESTAMENT

1 Quoted in *The Disinherited Mind* by Erich Heller (Bowes and Bowes, London and Barnes and Noble, New York, 1971).

2 cf. R. de Vaux, *The Early History of Israel* (Darton, Longman and Todd, 1978).

3 1 Samuel 28:13.

4 Psalm 95:3.

5 Psalm 96:5.

6 Exodus 4:24.

7 2 Samuel 6:7.

8 Exodus 12:29.

9 Deuteronomy 2:34. cf. 1 Samuel 15:3.

10 Matthew 25:31–46.

11 According to the generally accepted theory of four sources for the early history of Israel (1) J – the Jahwist account, using the name of Jahweh (or Yahveh) for God, composed in the ninth century (2) E – the Elohist account, using the name of Elohim for God, and written in the eighth century (3) D – the author of Deuteronomy, writing in the seventh century (4) P – the priestly writer, responsible for the final redaction in the sixth century. This theory may not be exact, but it probably represents the main lines of the development of the Old Testament.

12 2 Samuel 7:1–17.

13 cf. Ezekiel 37:24–5.

14 Luke 1:32–3.

II

THE MYTH OF THE NEW CREATION

15 Revelation 21:1.

16 Ephesians 1:10.

17 The texts are to be found in *Evolution and Theology* by E. C. Messenger.

18 Genesis 2:2.

19 Genesis 28:16–17.

20 Hebrews 11:16.

21 Isaiah 65:17–18.

22 Romans 8:19–21.

23 Revelation 21:5.

24 Revelation 21:4.
25 2 Peter 3:13.

III

THE MYTH OF PARADISE LOST

26 Genesis 2:8.
27 Genesis 2:9.
28 Genesis 2:7.
29 cf. *The Abolition of Man* by C. S. Lewis, (Geoffrey Bles, 1962, page 52 and Fount Paperbacks, 1978, page 46).
30 Genesis 3:5.
31 Genesis 3:12.
32 John 3:14.
33 Genesis 1:27.
34 Genesis 3:17.
35 Genesis 3:16.

IV

THE MYTH OF THE PROMISED LAND

36 Genesis 12:1.
37 Genesis 3:24.
38 Romans 5:14.
39 Ephesians 4:13.
40 Genesis 4:2.
41 cf. Hebrews 11:9.
42 cf. Hebrews 11:10.
43 Genesis 12:3.
44 Genesis 26:2–3.
45 Genesis 35:9–12.
46 Exodus 6:6–8.
47 Joshua 1:6.
48 Jeremiah 31:31–33.
49 Ezekiel 36:26.
50 Ezekiel 37:14.
51 Isaiah 65:17–18.

Notes

52 The Gospel of Thomas 22.
53 cf. Ezekiel 36:28.
54 Hebrews 8:5.
55 Hebrews 11:8, 15–16.
56 Isaiah 62:4–5.

V

THE MYTH OF THE EXODUS

57 2 Peter 2:5.
58 1 Corinthians 10:2.
59 Exodus 40:38.
60 1 Kings 8:10–11.
61 Ezekiel 43:2–5.
62 Mark 9:7.
63 Acts 1:9.
64 Exodus 24:16–18.
65 The doctrine of Gregory of Nyssa is to be found mainly in the *Life of Moses*, translated in Classics of Western Spirituality, published by the Paulist Press, 1978. The most profound study that I know of his mystical doctrine is that of Jean Daniélou in *Platonisme et Théologie Mystique* (Paris, 1944).
66 John 3:5.
67 John 4:14.
68 Exodus 24:8.
69 John 13:1.
70 Exodus 33:18.
71 John 17:5.
72 Brihadaranyaka Upanishad 1:3:27.
73 John 14:2.
74 John 17:24.
75 John 17:21.

212

Notes

VI

THE MYTH OF THE MESSIAH AND HIS KINGDOM

76 2 Samuel 7:13–14.
77 cf. Ezekiel 37:21–25.
78 Psalm 2:7.
79 Psalm 110:1.
80 cf. Genesis 14:18.
81 Psalm 110:4.
82 Isaiah 53:4–5.
83 John 10:11.
84 Daniel 7:13.
85 Mark 14:62.
86 Ezekiel 2:1, etc.
87 Psalm 8:4.
88 Rig Veda 10:90
89 cf. *De L'Homme Universel* by Titus Burckhardt (Collection Soufisme, Lyon, 1953).
90 cf. *Buddhist Texts* by Edward Conze, pages 143–4 and 181–4 (Cassirer, Oxford, 1954).
91 John 12:34.
92 1 Corinthians 15:47.
93 1 Corinthians 15:49.
94 Luke 9:58.
95 Mark 14:62.
96 Hebrews 9:11–12.
97 cf. Matthew 25, Revelation 19:7.
98 Acts 1:6.
99 Matthew 20:21.
100 Micah 4:2–3.
101 Isaiah 9:7.
102 Isaiah 11:1–6.
103 Daniel 7:14.

Notes

VII

THE MYTH OF THE NEW JERUSALEM AND THE
CITY OF GOD

104 cf. 1 Samuel 8:4–22.
105 1 Samuel 10:17–19.
106 2 Samuel 7:6.
107 Acts 2:46.
108 cf. Deuteronomy 4:1–2.
109 Deuteronomy 6:8–9.
110 cf. Deuteronomy 29:29.
111 Mark 2:27.
112 Matthew 22:37–40.
113 Acts 22:3.
114 cf. Romans 6:5–6.
115 Mark 13:1–2.
116 1 Kings 8:20.
117 2 Kings 25:8–9.
118 cf. Ezra 3:7.
119 Psalm 2:6.
120 Psalm 48:1–2.
121 Psalm 50:2.
122 Psalm 87:4–6.
123 Isaiah 62:3.
124 Isaiah 65:17–18.
125 Matthew 23:37.
126 John 4:21–23.
127 Hebrews 8:2–5.
128 Hebrews 9:11.
129 Revelation 21:2.
130 Revelation 21:3.
131 Revelation 21:22–23.
132 Katha Upanishad 5:15.
133 Koran 55:26.

Notes

IV

The Christian Revelation

I

THE WAY OF INTUITIVE WISDOM

1 *Tao Te Ching* 6, 10 and 16. From *The Wisdom of China* by Lin Yutang (Michael Joseph, London).

2 D. H. Lawrence, *Apocalypse*.

3 Genesis 4:1.

4 The most profound study of sexual love that I know is that of Mary and Robert Joyce in *New Dynamics in Sexual Love* (St John's, Collegeville, USA, 1970).

5 In *Creative Intuition in Art and Poetry* by J. Maritain (Meridian Books, New York, 1954), especially chapter 3, 'The Pre-conscious life of the Intellect', and chapter 4, 'Creative Intuition and Poetic Knowledge', to which I owe much of my understanding of the nature of intuitive knowledge.

6 *Paradiso*, 33, translated by Barbara Reynolds (Penguin Classics).

7 Eckhart, *Sermon*, 90.

8 Katha Upanishad 2:23.

II

THE MYTH OF CHRIST

9 The deepest study of the Hindu gods that I know is that of Alain Daniélou in *Hindu Polytheism* (Routledge and Kegan Paul, London, 1964).

10 Bhagavad Gita 4:7.

11 Acts 2:4.

12 Acts 2:4.

13 Ephesians 1:10 (as translated by Ronald Knox); literally, 'as a plan for the fullness of time'.

14 cf. C. H. Dodd, *The Apostolic Preaching and its Development* (Hodder

and Stoughton, London, 1936), still the most authoritative work of its kind that I know.

15 Acts 2:21, quoting the prophet Joel.
16 Wisdom of Solomon 1:7.
17 Acts 2:36.
18 Psalm 2:7.
19 Daniel 7:13.
20 cf. Deuteronomy 18:13.
21 Hebrews 8:1.
22 John 1:1.
23 Isaiah 7:14.
24 Luke 2:52.
25 Luke 22:44.
26 Mark 15:34, Matthew 27:46.
27 cf. C. H. Dodd *The Interpretation of the Fourth Gospel* (Cambridge University Press, 1953), and *Tradition in the Fourth Gospel*. Also Raymond Brown in his commentary on St John's Gospel in the Anchor Bible (Chapman and Hall, London, 1971).
28 cf. Acts 4:26–7.
29 Bhagavad Gita 10:3.
30 Bhagavad Gita 10:11.
31 Wisdom of Solomon 7:26–7.
32 Sirach 24:3.

III

THE MYTH OF THE CHURCH

33 *Shepherd of Hermas*, 2:24.
34 Ephesians 1:22–3.
35 1 Corinthians 15:45.
36 John 1:14.
37 Mark 1:15.
38 Colossians 3:3.
39 1 Corinthians 13:12.
40 Galatians 6:15.

Index

Abel, 124
Aborigines, Australian, 30, 88, 202
Abraham, 110; and promise to mankind, 125, 126, 130, 176
absolute, the, 101, 107
Adam, 123–4, 193, 195, 196; and Eve, 31, 105, 159; Kadmon, 14, 70, 140; Noah: new, 133, second, 123, 141, 193, 196
Advaita school (non-duality), 79, 85, 90, 92
Aeschylus, 171
Africa, tribal peoples of, 88, 152, 158, 159
Agni, 81
agnosticism, 202
agriculture, 124
Alexandria, school of, 112–13, 130
Al Ghazali, 21
Allah, 42
alternative society, 40–1
ananda; bliss consciousness, 94, 95; and Christian Trinity, 190. *See Saccidananda*
angels, 49, 56, 107; good and evil, 73–4
animal, the, 66
Antioch, school of, 112
Arabia, 100
Aristotle, 71, 72, 126; body-soul concept, 57; principle of potentiality, 53, 74
art, 164, 165
Ascent into heaven; of Jesus, 32, 34, 135, 175; of Pharaoh, 175
Ashram, 44
Asia, 88, 157
asuras, 73, 107
atheism, 202
atman, 49, 58
Atman, 26, 27, 59, 60, 62, 66, 68; active

principle of form, 83; and Brahman, 86–7, 89; and Christian Trinity, 190–1; and Krishna, 86–7; one with Brahman and Purusha, 75–6, 78, 102, 174
Attis, 175
Augustine, St, 93; *City of God*, 124–5; on creation of world, 113
Augustus, Emperor, 32
Aurobindo, Sri, 50–1, 62, 63, 172
avataras, 175, 176
avidya (ignorance), 17, 29, 58, 74
avyakta (the unmanifest), 71, 74

Babel, tower of, 105
Babylon, 109, 124, 143
Bangalore, 12, 18
baptism, 37–8, 69, 201; symbols of, 132 3, 136
Barfield, Owen, 49–50
Belur, temples at, 13–14
Bhagavad Gita, 17, 88, 107, 190; and concept of personal God, 86–7; and divine love, 94; language of, 102
Bhagavan, 81
bhakti (devotion), 94, 174
Bible, 21, 24, 43, 55, 180–1; allegorical meaning, 110–11; language, 102–3; mythology and symbolism, 31–4; poetry of, 48; and the Reformation, 198; story of mankind in relation to God, 123–4, 196; and theme of failure of human effort, 132
Blake, William, 8, 103
Bodhisattva, 61
Bombay, 8, 10, 11
Book of the Dove, The (Bar Hebraeus), 21

Index

Index

Earth, worship of, 124

East, the; and contemplative dimension of human existence, 10–11; and dominance of unconscious mind, 8–9; marriage with West, 151, 165, 203, 204

Eckhart, Meister, 84, 168

ecumenism, 23, 24–5, 198

Eden, Garden of, 129; myth of, 117–23

Egypt, 68, 124, 185, 197; symbolism in Exodus, 133–4

Eliade, Mircea, 206

Elohim, 106, 118

Endor, witch of, 106

energy; alternative, 40; reflection of divine, 96

enlightenment, 59

episcopacy, 37, 200, 201

Eskimos, 202

'eternal return', cosmic myth of, 112, 180

Eucharist, 18, 136, 201

Euripides, 171

Eve, 31, 105, 159

evil, 39

Exodus, the, 106, 109, 110; myth and symbolism, 133–8

Ezekiel, 135, 140

faith; function of intuitive mind, 199; leap of, 75–6, 102

Fall of Man, 29, 30, 31, 110, 175, 195; reversal of effects, 130

Fathers of the Church, 57, 85, 110, 134–5, 189

feminine; dominant in Eastern mind, 8, 9; and domination of masculine, 151–2; the eternal, 192; 'marriage' with masculine, 129–30, 159, 165; and masculine in human being, 9, 54–5, 165

Flood, the, 105, 110, 132

form, matter and, 53–4

'fourth' state, 94. See turiya

Francis of Sales, St, 76

Freud, Sigmund, 161

Gandhi, Mahatma, 10, 139, 172

Ganesh, 173, 174

Gayatri mantra, 56

Genesis, Book of, 54, 132; creation story, 105, 110, 111–12; Garden of Eden, 117–23

godhead; non-dual nature, 98–9;

participation in inner life of, 100

God; action and revelation in history, 110–11, 176, 177; both Father and Mother, 55, 191; conceived as Person, 26; divine archetype, 84–5; dynamism of love in, 95–7; expression in analogical terms, 101; immanence, 11, 16–17, 25–6, 83–4, 85–6; Incarnation, 17; infinite holiness, 21, 22; and language of imagination, 103–4; plan for whole creation, 112; rejection by West, 16; revelation to all men, 38; sign for ultimate Truth, 42; transcendence, 16, 25–6, 83; as ultimate Reality, 25, 26–7; Upanishads' and Gita's concept of personal, 79, 87; wrathful and terrible aspect, 107–8. See also absolute; Reality, ultimate

gods; and cosmic powers, 49, 72–3; Hindu, 172–4; subjection to supreme being of oriental, 16; of Vedas, 81. See also devas

Goethe, Wolfgang, 103, 163

Golden String, The (Griffiths), 7, 46

grace, 76, 94, 108

Granth Sahib, 24

Great Mother (Devi), 173, 192

Greece, 100

Greek tragedy, 61, 163, 171, 172

Gregory of Nyssa, 113, 135, 136

Halebid, temple at, 13–14

Hanuman, 13, 173, 174

Hara, 79

heaven, 39, 109, 112

Hebrews, Letter to the, 130–1, 148

Heisenberg, Werner, 28, 52

hell, 39, 108–9

Herod the Great, 147

Hinduism, 12, 16, 42, 51, 149, 152, 202, 203; the Cosmic Religion, 14; and demythologization, 174–5; divisions and harmony in, 22; the 'eternal' religion, 177; immanence and transcendence of God in, 16–17, 25–6, 83, 86–7; and knowledge of the Self, 91; renaissance, 158, 172–3; and 'terrible' aspect of God, 108; and world of myth, 172–5

history, 180

Holy Spirit: as Ananda and Atman, 190–1; bliss of, 44; coming of, 43; and

Index

Holy Spirit [*contd.*]
  communion of love, 35; feminine aspect
  of godhead, 55, 99, 191–2, 193; and
  guidance of different churches, 37;
  outpouring at Pentecost, 35–6, 179, 182
Homer, 32, 48, 61, 86, 105, 163, 172; and
  myth, 171

idealism, 57
Iliad (Homer), 32, 105
imagination; ancient man and world of,
  48–9, 59–60, 67; expression in symbols,
  50, 59; language of, 103–4, 163; marriage
  with reason, 61, 166; and myth, 49, 170;
  poetic, 163–4
India, 7–11, 100, 150, 181, 197; Church in,
  11, 19–20; poverty and simplicity in,
  12–13, 18–19; primeval religion in, 31;
  and primordial truth, 47; and sacredness
  of created things, 15; 'wisdom' of, 68
Indians, American, 30, 88, 202
Indra, 106
industrialism, 9–10, 151
Inquisition, 198
intellect, active and passive, 154–7, 162,
  166. *See also* imagination, mind, reason
intelligences, 72
intolerance, 22
intuition; embryonic thought, 60–1;
  feminine power of mind, 152; imaginative sphere, 162; knowledge from mind's
  reflection on itself, 153–5, 156–8;
  'marriage' with reason, 10, 121, 159,
  165–6, 199; and the mystic, 167; and
  myth, 170; and sex, 159–61
Isa Upanishad, 79
Isaac, 110, 126
Isaiah, 128, 131, 142, 147, 186
Islam, 11, 42, 51, 68, 91; and concept of
  wrathful deity, 108; and Syrian
  Christianity, 21; and Universal Man, 14,
  70, 140
Israel; as 'bride' of Yahweh, 186; cultural
  limitations, 197; and myth of Messiah,
  138–43; as people of God, 124–6, 143–4;
  and Suffering Servant, 139, 141;
  transformation of external religion,
  127–8

Jacob, 110, 115, 126
Jainism, 14, 59

Japan, 68
Jaspers, Karl, 59
Jerusalem; as city of God, 116, 142, 147–8;
  the new, 115, 128, 147, 148
Jesus Christ; Ascension, 32, 34, 135, 175;
  and Christian myth, 175; consummation
  of union of God with man in, 194–5;
  cosmic Lord, 196; death, 32, 34, 137–8,
  175, 179, 182, 188; 'divinity' of, 186–7;
  faith in, 37–8; and foundation of Church,
  201; and fulfilment of destiny of Man,
  187; the 'great Sannyasi', 43; in history,
  32, 179, 180; and Holy Spirit, 189, 191;
  intuitive awareness, 189; and Jewish law,
  145–6; lament over Jerusalem, 147–8; as
  Lord, 182, 183; as man, 33; manifestation
  of divine Reality in, 34; as Messiah, 61,
  139, 182, 188–9; miracles, 34, 184; and
  Mystical Body doctrine, 93, 100; and
  Old Testament myth, 105; parables, 39,
  108–9; Prophet, Priest, Mediator, 183;
  relationship to Father, 33, 35, 99–100,
  187, 191; Resurrection, 32, 34, 36–7, 43,
  175, 183–4, 186, 188, 195; Second Adam,
  141; second coming, 34, 36–7, 175, 203,
  204; a 'sign' of God, 42; sojourn in
  desert, 134; Son of God, 32, 33, 139, 141,
  182, 183, 186; Son of Man, 14, 32, 140–1,
  183; as Suffering Servant, 139, 141;
  transfiguration, 135; Virgin Birth, 32, 34,
  184, 185, 186; Word of God, 38, 183, 187
jivatman (human spirit), 76, 77
John, St, Apostle, 189
John the Baptist, 134
John Chrysostom, St, 112
John, Gospel of St, 33, 99, 121, 137, 189
Joseph, 126
Joshua, 126, 127
Judaism, 11; and concept of wrathful
  deity, 107–8; *See also* Israel
Jung, C. G., 9, 153–4, 162
Jupiter, 106

Kali, 108
Katha Upanishad, 68–9, 71, 74–6
Keats, John, 46, 47, 48, 60, 156
Kerala, 18–21, 23
King, Martin Luther, 139
Kingdom of God, 32, 43, 44, 142–3, 181,
  196
Koran, 21, 24, 103

220

Index

Krishna, 61, 173–4, 176, 180; identical with Brahman and Atman, 86–7, 107
Kurisumala Ashram, 23, 24

language, 31, 50, 62, 79, 101–2
law, Jewish, 127, 145–6
Lawrence, D. H., 158
Le Saux, Father, 23, 205
Lewis, C. S., 49
liberation, 29, 181
lingam, 14, 82
liturgy, Syrian, 21
love; commandments of, 146; communion of, 35; ecstasy of, 161–2; mystical, 96–7, 161; sexual, 95–6, 160–1; and wrath in deity, 108
Luke, Gospel of St, 188

magic, 120, 185
Mahabharata, 14, 61, 105
Mahanjadaro, 81
mahat (Great Self), 71–3, 74
man; archetypal, 14, 70 140; body, soul and spirit, 57–8, 61–2, 118, 122, 199; created in harmony with nature, 118, 120, 122, 129; final term of evolution, 113–14; image and son of God, 35, 85, 122, 193; 'schizophrenia' in Western, 57; self-consciousness in, 66–7; and woman, 164–5
manas (mind), 71
Manikkai Vasagar, 24
mankind; division of, 124–5; liberation of, 126
Maritain, Jacques, 154, 163
Mary, 110, 192
masculine, the; domination in West, 8, 9, 151–2, 164; and feminine in human being, 9, 54–5, 165; 'marriage' with feminine, 129–30, 159, 165
materialism, 27–8, 57
matter; consciousness latent in, 52–3, 66, 184–5, 194; and form, 53–4; interpenetration with mind, 29, 184; potentiality, 53, 170
maya (illusion), 29, 54, 58–9, 74; world of experience regarded as, 17, 30, 72, 91, 176
medicine, Western, 52
meditation, 24, 58, 69, 174; communion with Purusha, 74–5; and revelation of

Brahman and Atman, 27, 89
Melchizedek, 139
Mesopotamia, 68
Messiah and his Kingdom, myth of, 110, 138–43, 175
metanoia, 68, 203
Micah, 142
Middle Ages, 47, 57, 151
Milton, John, 73
mind; communion of intuitive and rational, 129–30; conscious and unconscious, 8–9; imaginative, 164; interpenetration with matter, 29, 184; intuitive, 50, 169–70; myth expression of intuitive, 170; rational, 8, 9, 27, 50, 58, 90–1, 92, 156, 164, 165, 169. *See also* intuition, reason
miracles, 34, 184–5
Mitra, 81
moksha (liberation), 29
monasticism, 41–2
Monchanin, Father Jules, 23, 205
Monophysitism, 20
Moses, 106, 107, 110, 121, 137, 176; figure of Saviour, 133; Law given to, 145; on Mount Sinai, 136; and renewal of promise to Abraham, 126
Murray, Gilbert, 171
Muslim religion, 149, 203. *See* Islam
Mysore State, temples in, 13–14
mystical experience, 167, 169, 174–5; Christian, 178–80; Hindu, 177–8, 179–80; and language of sexual union, 161
myth, 89, 128, 202; and the Bible, 31–3; Christian: historic, 175–6; displacement by science and reason, 171; evolution in Siva and Krishna, 81–2, 86; expression of one Reality, 29–30, 43, 104; Hindu: cosmic and cyclic, 172–6; and imagination, 49, 181–2; place in human evolution, 170–1; reconciliation of Hindu and Christian, 177; religious doctrine expression of, 148–9; threefold meaning, 105

Nachiketas, 69
nature; forces of, 129, 159; immanence of Spirit in, 193; and man, 118, 120, 122, 129–30
Neo-Platonism, 21, 26

221

Index

Nestorianism, 19, 20
New Testament, 33, 104, 108, 112, 202; on characteristics of Messiah's kingdom, 143; and Church organization, 36–7, 200–1; on heaven and hell, 39; and question of Jewish law, 145; symbolic interpretation of Old Testament, 135
Newman, Cardinal J. H., 103
Nicaea, Council of, 40
Nirvana, 26, 29
Noah, 88, 110, 133
non-duality, experience of, 92–3, 177

Odyssey (Homer), 105
Old Testament; mythology of, 103, 104–5, 109–11, 191–2; and New Testament, 112, 135; and Wisdom, 191
Origen, 111, 112, 135, 136
Osiris, 175
Otto, Rudolf, 106

Panikkar, Dr R., 13, 30, 205
Panis, 56–7
pantheism, 16
papacy, 37, 200, 201
Parabrahman, 87
Paradise, 31, 123, 130, 175
Paradise Lost (Milton), 73
Paramatman; highest self, 87; and *jivatman*, 76, 77
paravidya (knowledge), 17
Passover, 107, 137, 145
patriarchs, Hebrew, 105–6, 110
Paul, St, 11, 134, 203; on Adam, 124; Christ as second Adam, 141; on cloud and Red Sea, 135; on common basis of faith, 38; on consummation of creation, 112, 195; on cosmic powers, 16, 56, 72, 207; Cosmic Revelation through creation, 88; immanence of God, 25–6, 84; on Jewish law, 146; man as body, soul and spirit, 57–8, 76–7; on new creation, 115–16; on passage of death, 203; on promise to Abraham, 125; on Spirit of God, 99–100
Peace, self of, 75
Pentecost, 35–6, 179, 181, 182, 183, 196
Persia, 19, 68, 197
person, human, 72, 93
Peter, St, Apostle, 201
Peter, Second Letter of St, 37, 117

Philo the Jew, 135
philosophy; Greek, 59, 151, 153, 198; Scholastic, 152–3; Western, 47, 57
physics, modern, 28, 52, 80
Plato, 47, 72, 130, 168, 178, 198
Pleroma, 195
Plotinus, 75, 100, 178
pneuma, 49, 58, 76–7, 190
Poetic Diction (Barfield), 49
poetry, 48, 61, 166, 174; Dante's, 166; Homer's, 32, 48, 171; Wordsworth on, 157
Polynesian Islanders, 202
Pontius Pilate, 32, 177, 196
potentiality, principle of, 53–4, 74
powers, psychic, 185
Prajapati (the creator), 64–5
Prakriti; feminine principle, 53, 55; 'marriage' with *Purusha*, 29, 186, 194, 195; nature, 80, 159; principle of 'potentiality', 74
prayer, 89, 174, 200
Promised Land, myth of, 110, 123–8, 129, 130–1, 132, 175
prophets, Hebrew, 59, 61
psychoanalysis, 155
punishment, eternal, 38–9, 108–9
Purusha, 62, 102, 159, 174; and Christian Trinity, 190, 191; figure in Jain temples, 14; marriage with *Prakriti*, 29, 186, 194, 195; masculine, active principle, 53, 55; primeval man and cosmic person, 70–1, 140; one with Atman and Brahman, 75–6, 78, 87; and *Sakti*, 55, 193; transcendent, personal God, 80–1, 83, 87
Purushottman, 87, 89, 93, 190
Pygmies, African, 129

Radha, 173
Ram Mohan Roy, 172
Rama, 61, 173, 176, 180
Ramakrishna, 158, 172
Ramayana, 14, 61, 105
Reality, ultimate, 27, 28, 42, 64, 101; Bible record of events in light of, 32–3; perennial philosophy's vision, 100; Upanishads and, 68, 79. *See also* absolute, God
reason; development of, 30, 60–1, 62, 63, 64, 67; 'marriage' with imagination, 61, 166; 'marriage' with intuition, 10, 121,

222

Index

223

Index

Sufi mystics, 140, 178
Surya, 81
Sushupti, 54, 154
Svetasvatara Upanishad, 78, 86; and concept of personal God, 79, 81, 82–3; story of two birds, 76, 119
symbol, 43, 128

Tacitus, 177
Tagore, Rabindranath, 172
Tao, 26, 53
Tao of Physics, The (Capra), 28, 205
Tao Te Ching, 157
Taoism, 12, 16, 59, 152, 178, 202
technology, 9–10, 125, 151
Temple, the, 110, 127, 135, 144, 147
theology, 11, 21, 47, 198
Third World, 41
Thomas, St, Apostle, 19
Thomas Aquinas, St, 43, 71, 104; angels in theology of, 56; God 'in' all things, 83–4; matter and form, 53; philosophy, 153
Tillich, Paul, 26
Tirumandiram, 82
Tolstoy, Leo, 32, 163
Trinity, the; doctrine of, 189–90; Holy Spirit as feminine aspect, 55, 99, 191–2; presence of, 84; and relationship of co-inherence, 98–100; *Saccidananda* as symbol of, 23, 190
truth, 25, 31
Truth, ultimate, 33–4, 202–3
turiya ('fourth state'), 65–6, 94

unconscious, the, 8, 54, 153–4, 162, 170
universe; Buddhist 'insubstantiality', 52; Newtonian, 28, 51–2; sacredness removed by Western man, 15; threefold nature of, 51, 53, 57, 71, 183–4; as unity, 30, 63, 70
Upanishads, 31, 59–60, 134, 138, 148, 174, 189; concept of personal God in, 78–9, 87; and cosmic unity, 89; and experience of ultimate Reality, 27; and immanence of God, 25; language of, 102; and non-duality, 90; and reality of material world, 17; and transformation of external religion, 127–8; wisdom of, 59, 61, 88
Uzzah, 107

Vala, 56
Vedanta, 7, 23, 59, 92; doctrine of, 71–2, 88; study of Reality in, 31
Vedas, 24, 31, 47–8, 50–1, 59–60, 61; doctrine of, 88; gods of, 56, 81, 172; language, 102, 103, multiple symbolism, 56–7; and mystical experience, 174; and threefold nature of world, 51, 57
Vedic myth, 51, 55–7, 207
Vico, Giambattista, 48, 206
Virgil, 32, 69, 163, 165
virgin birth, 32, 34, 175, 184
Vishnu, 86, 173–4
Visistadvaita school, 79
Vivekananda, 172
Void, the, 26, 75. *See* Nirvana
Vritra, 56

War and Peace (Tolstoy), 32
water, symbolism of, 132–3
West, the; and awareness of God, 11; dominance of conscious mind, 8; 'marriage' with East, 8, 151, 165, 203, 204
Western man, 151, 200
Wisdom, feminine, 55, 191
witchcraft, 165
women; liberation, 122; suppression in Church, 199
words, symbolism of, 62
Wordsmith, William, 46, 48, 102, 157, 160, 161
world; the 'becoming' of God, 192–3; future of, 9; Hindu denial of reality, 17; reflection of ultimate Reality, 95; threefold nature of, 51, 79–80, 87, 183–4. *See also* universe
worship, 147–9

Yahweh, 17, 42, 118, 147; as God of Israel, 106–7, 186; holiness and daemonic aspect, 107–8
Yama, 69
Yang and Yin, 10, 53
Yoga, 23, 86, 155
yoni, 14

Zerubbabel, 147
Zeus, 106
Zoroastrianism, 59